WORDS THAT HURT WORDS THAT HEAL

Carole Mayhall

NAVPRESS

A MINISTRY OF THE NAVIGATORS
P.O. BOX 35001, COLORADO SPRINGS, COLORADO 80935

The Navigators is an international Christian organization.
Our mission is to reach, disciple, and equip people to know
Christ and to make Him known through successive genera-
tions. We envision multitudes of diverse people in the United
States and every other nation who have a passionate love
for Christ, live a lifestyle of sharing Christ's love, and multi-
ply spiritual laborers among those without Christ.

NavPress is the publishing ministry of The Navigators.
NavPress publications help believers learn biblical truth and
apply what they learn to their lives and ministries. Our mission is to stimulate spiritual formation among our readers.

Library of Congress Catalog Card Number:
    86-61136
ISBN 08910-91793

Unless otherwise identified, all Scripture quotations are from
the *Holy Bible: New International Version* (NIV). Copyright ©
1973, 1978, 1984, International Bible Society. Used by permission of Zondervan Bible Publishers. Other versions used
include: the *Revised Standard Version* Bible (RSV), copy-
righted 1946, 1952, © 1971, 1973; the *New American
Standard Bible* (NASB), © The Lockman Foundation 1960,
1962, 1963, 1968, 1971, 1972, 1973, 1975, 1977; the
Amplified New Testament (AMP), © The Lockman
Foundation 1954, 1958; the *New King James Version*
(NKJV), copyright © 1979, 1980, 1982, Thomas Nelson Inc.,
Publishers; the *New Testament in Modern English* (Revised
Edition), J. B. Phillips Translator, (PH) © J. B. Phillips 1958,
1960, 1972, used by permission of Macmillan Publishing
Company; *The Living Bible* (TLB), © 1971, used by permis-
sion of Tyndale House Publishers, Inc., Wheaton, IL 60189,
all rights reserved; and the *Modern Language Bible: The
Berkeley Version in Modern English* (MLB), copyright © 1945,
1959, 1969 by Zondervan Publishing House, and used by
permission.

Mayhall, Carole.
    Words that hurt, words that heal / by Carole Mayhall.
    108 p. ; 23 cm.
    ISBN 0-89109-543-8 :
    1. Christian life. 2. Conduct of life. I. Title.
    BV4501.2.M426   1986
    241/.672 19   86-61136
                                                    CIP

Printed in the United States of America

13 14 15 16 17 18 19 20 21 / 00 99 98 97 96

Contents

To Jack

Friend-husband
Counselor
Lover
Companion

One who has shown me the meaning
of self-control—
yes, of tongue-control

With my deepest gratitude

Author

Carole Mayhall is a popular Christian communicator. She has traveled throughout the world speaking to women at seminars and conferences on the subject of discipleship.

Carole is a graduate of Wheaton College, with a degree in Christian Education. She and her husband, Jack, have served in the Navigator ministry for many years. Jack is the director of the Marriage and Family Discipleship Department for The Navigators.

The Mayhalls live in Colorado Springs, Colorado.

Carol has also written *When God Whispers* and with Jack has coauthored *Marriage Takes More Than Love.*

WHEN A GOOD MAN SPEAKS,
HE IS WORTH LISTENING TO,
BUT THE WORDS OF FOOLS
ARE A DIME A DOZEN.

PROVERBS 10:20, TLB

Preface

WARNING! DO NOT READ THIS BOOK—unless, of course, you want God to teach you, as He is teaching me, some vital issues about our speech. That is what this book is all about. I trust it will be a straightforward handling of a devious matter—our tongue. James tells us that the tongue is like the bit in a horse's mouth; if we control the bit, we control the horse (see James 3:3).

The tongue is the biggest, littlest bit we possess. And God has a great deal to say about this member—both positive and negative.

May God's Spirit convict you and me as we look into what to say, how to say it, when to speak and when not to speak—issues that are especially hard for women. May we bring our tongues to the place where they glorify God.

Introduction
COMMITMENT COMES FIRST

Six hundred women swarmed into the hive-shaped banquet hall and fluttered to rest. The buzzing became a low hum and finally stilled as we waited for the evening session of the conference to begin.

Dennis was an eloquent speaker, and challenged us with story after story of taking the Bible to East Asia. His climaxing illustration left me shaken.

On a recent visit to an Asian church, he sat next to a small woman whose hands were so crippled she could not hold the hymn book. Following the service, he turned to her and asked, "Do you have a Bible?"

"No," she said softly.

"Would you like to have one?" he queried.

"Oh, yes!" Her face brightened.

"If you will come back to my hotel, I will give you one," offered Dennis.

As they walked back to his hotel, Dennis asked the diminutive woman about her hands. She told him the following story.

"When the soldiers were searching for all Bibles, hymn books, and religious material, they came to my door. I had hidden my Bible under the cold ashes of my stove, but they knew all the places to look. As they were taking my Bible from my house, I grabbed it and said, 'Oh, please don't take my Bible. It's all that I have to tell me about my Jesus.'

"The men said, 'It's nothing but a book of fables. Give it to us, old woman.'

"But again I cried, 'Oh, please don't take it. It's all that I have that tells me about my Jesus.'"

The woman said they took her outside, stripped her, and put her up on a platform to shame her before the crowds. For four hours she sat with the Bible clutched to her naked breast, head down as the crowds mocked and spit on her. They thought she was ashamed, but she was praying.

She continued, "After four hours they again tried to take my Bible, but I clung to it and said, 'Please don't take it. It's all that I have that tells me about my Jesus.'"

Angrily they spread her out in the dirt with hands clasped and arms stretched over her head and beat her hands with a hammer until they were nothing but pulp. To this day she cannot even feed herself.

As I listened to this story, I was deeply touched. Dennis was totally committed to taking the Word of God to dangerous places. The woman was totally committed to Christ and to His Word.

The speaker the next morning was a sweet-faced woman from JAARS (Jungle Aviation and Radio Service), a branch of Wycliffe Bible Translators. Beverly told of being a homemaker in Kansas when, one evening, a call for dedication was given at their church missions conference. She and her husband, their three small children between them, walked down the aisle and said to the Lord, "Anywhere, anytime, and anything, Lord."

Two years later, Beverly walked into a tarpaper shack that was to be her home in Papua New Guinea. It had a two-foot separation between the walls and roof, allowing anything to come and go. She looked around and whispered, "I didn't mean this, Lord."

She cried for two weeks, and when her husband asked if she wanted to go home, she said yes. But the Lord gently loved her until she could say again, "Anywhere, anytime, anything, Lord." She and her husband were privileged to see many come out of the darkness into God's light.

Seven years later, Beverly waved goodbye to her only son returning to college in the United States. In her heart she cried, "I didn't mean this, Lord." But again, after a struggle, she trusted God to care for her son while he was half a world away.

Two years later her family was reunited when they were transferred to North Carolina where her husband was to train other aircraft mechanics at the JAARS base. Her son planned to become a pilot for the jungle aviation program.

One night Bev answered the insistent ringing of the telephone. A doctor from a local hospital urged, "Come quickly. There's been an auto accident." Bev and her husband rushed to the hospital. The doctor met them, and with voice breaking he said, "Your son's girl friend is in x-ray right now—we think she is going to make it. But . . . I'm sorry to tell you that your son did not."

Into Bev's mind flashed the image of a young couple, their three small children between them, walking down the aisle of a church and saying, "Anywhere, anytime, anything, Lord." And the enemy of her soul taunted, "See! See what God does when you give everything to Him?" Her heart cried in agony, "Oh, I didn't mean this, Lord."

Then quietly to her heart the Lord said, "Beverly, I gave My only Son for you. Are you willing to let yours go to be with Me?" And she was able to respond, "Anywhere, anytime, anything, Lord."

Beverly's face was illuminated from within as she told her story and then sang a beautiful song of praise to God.

I slipped away from the crowd and went back to my room. There I wept and cried out to God. I was weeping for the little woman with crippled hands. I was weeping for Beverly's loss. But I was also weeping for myself. You see, I was to be the next speaker.

I prayed, "Lord, what in the world am I doing here? Dennis and Bev and the little woman are extraordinary people and have had extraordinary experiences. They are totally committed to You, and their faces and lives reflect that. But then there's me! I've never lived in a tarpaper shack. I've never taught savages. I've never been beaten because of my love for Your Word. Lord, I'm supposed to speak after them? I don't deserve to sit on the same platform. I am so . . . so ordinary."

The Lord spoke firmly to my heart. He said, "That's true. You are."

In an instant, I knew what He was saying. Yes, I am ordinary. But we ordinary people have an extraordinary call to an extraordinary God who calls each of us to total commitment. He has called me to respond, "Anywhere, anytime, anything." And whether I live in a tarpaper shack in a jungle or in a home in Colorado, whether I minister to savages or my neighbors, whether I suffer physically or am spared pain matters not. It is my *heart* commitment that is imperative, my willingness to be totally His—anywhere, anytime, and in anything.

Many Christ-ones merely want involvement—and a small piece of it at that—in Christianity. God wants total commitment. He wants us to be wholehearted. Sold out. Willing to pay the price of being *disciples*.

The purpose of our lives is *to know God*. At the end of his life, the Apostle Paul still desired this at an ever deeper level:

> [For my determined purpose is] that I may know Him—that I may progressively become more deeply and intimately acquainted with Him, perceiving and recognizing and understanding [the wonders of His Person] more strongly and more clearly. And that I may in that same way come to know the power outflowing from His resurrection [which it exerts over believers]; and that I may so share His sufferings as to be continually transformed [in spirit into His likeness even] to His death. (Philippians 3:10, AMP)

This means commitment to God and to His Word with our whole being. It has been said that the Christian life is one big YES and a lot of little uh-huh's—YES when we ask Christ into our lives to be our Savior and uh-huh in the multitude of lordship decisions we make through the years. Perhaps there will be one time when we say, "Anywhere, anytime, anything, Lord," and like Beverly, God will reveal an area we didn't know existed until the test comes and we say, "Uh-huh" in that area.

Where do we begin?

Perhaps we begin by memorizing Romans 12:1-2. The Phillips paraphrase is especially thought-provoking:

> With eyes wide open to the mercies of God, I beg you, my brothers, as an act of intelligent worship, to give him your bodies, as a living sacrifice, consecrated to him and acceptable by him. Don't let the world around you squeeze you into its own mould, but let God re-make you so that your whole attitude of mind is changed. Thus you will prove in practice that the will of [God is] good, acceptable to him and perfect.

Our bodies are to be "living sacrifices" because of God's mercy to us—His love—and the fact that His plan for us is *good* and will make us mature.

What is it that we hold back? Perhaps it's the little things we don't think a lot about, like watching too much television and wasting precious hours that belong to God. Or not setting a consistent time to spend with God each day or taking time for deep Bible study. Perhaps it is a fruit of the spirit (patience? self-control?) that we know needs work, but we fail to even ask God for creative ideas concerning it.

Or perhaps it is what comes out of our *mouths*. We may have many areas of life under the control of the Holy Spirit, but do we have that one?

During a retreat at which I spoke, I was handed a white 3-by-5 card that read, "Will you say a word on gossip, the tongue, building up the body? I'm so surprised by what I hear—even at this retreat among professing Christians. As one younger than the majority here, I must say I'm disappointed in my elders—those whom I expected to learn so much from by their mature example."

I winced at the words, and a cold shadow slipped over my spirit. It is amazing to me how careless and unconcerned we supposedly mature Christians are about what we say. We may have known God for ten or twenty or more years, yet still go about sinning with our tongues, completely insensitive to the fact we are grieving the Holy Spirit. His voice was quenched long ago by our habitual unconcern and unresponsiveness in this area.

It hurt to read a secular author's impression of a lot of Christians. In describing one of his characters in a novel, Ken Follett wrote, "He believed in Communism the way most people believed in God; He would not be greatly surprised or disappointed if he turned out to be wrong, and meanwhile it made little difference to the way he lived."[1]

Perhaps we should echo, "It makes little difference in the way we *talk*." Oh, hopefully, vulgar, offensive words are no longer in our vocabulary. We are offended if God's name is taken in vain. But we blissfully continue in gossip, in slander, in reckless, careless, idle speech that is *revolting* to God.

However, the results of having a tongue controlled by God are *spectacular*.

We will be encouragers. Many anxious hearts surround us. Burdens and hurts weigh heavily on loved ones' hearts. Proverbs 12:25 advises, "Anxious hearts are very heavy but a word of encouragement does wonders!" (TLB).

A second result is that *people will come to know God.* That's a promise! King David wrote, "He put a new song in my mouth, a hymn of praise to our God. Many will see and fear and put their trust in the LORD" (Psalm 40:3). What we say will be acceptable and pleasing to God.

A third result of having a tongue controlled by God is that *we will be offering sacrifices to God* Himself. Yes, amazing as it seems, our speech is a sacrifice to God: "Through Jesus, therefore, let us continually offer to God a sacrifice of praise—the fruit of lips that confess his name. And do not forget to do good and to share with others, for with such sacrifices God is pleased" (Hebrews 13:15-16).

Do you catch the significance of what this verse is teaching? Our words of praise (the fruit of our lips) are on a par with doing good and sharing with others. With all these "sacrifices" *God is pleased.* May I often find myself praying, "May the words of my mouth and the meditation of my heart be pleasing in your sight, O LORD, my Rock and my Redeemer" (Psalm 19:14).

God speaks a great deal about "the mouth of the righteous." And we are going to look into some of the whats and wherefores of our tongues. But perhaps we first need to look deep within our own hearts and ask God to sensitize us anew to His still small voice. We need to throw our hearts wide open to learning in this area what we may have ignored so long, and to pray with sincerity, "Lord, teach me what it means to have the mouth of the righteous. Teach me how it fits into total commitment. I want my mouth—my tongue and my words—to bring glory to You all the days of my life."

NOTES

1. Ken Follett, *Triple* (Boston: G. K. Hall, 1979), page 77. (Signet Books)

❧ 1 ❧
A Fountain or a Babbling Brook?

The young man came in looking as though he had just been touched with sunshine. Wonderingly he shook his head and said, "I don't think I've had more than twenty minutes with Bob since I've worked here—and those have been in two- and three-minute snatches when he's picked me up to ride a couple of blocks with him. But every time we've had a moment, he's shared something with me that was just what I needed." He was whistling softly as he turned to his desk.

I thought, *Imagine that! Only a couple of minutes of unplanned time. Yet Bob's words were a fountain of life.* Proverbs 10:11 came to mind: "The mouth of the righteous is a fountain of life."

I sighed. I'm afraid my words are more often like a babbling brook than a fountain of life. Sometimes I chatter away without thought or sensitivity. But since hearing that young man's statement, I have prayed often, "Please, Lord, make my mouth a fountain—a well—of life today."

A babbling brook runs on the surface, rushing helter-skelter over the rocks. A well runs deep, with substance.

Think back. Back to the last three conversations you have had with Christian friends apart from a Bible study or Sunday school class. I mean real conversations, not just "Hi-how-are-you" types. What were the subjects you talked about? Or can you remember?

The minute I meet some people, I know how the conversation is going to go. No matter how hard I try with some, a whirlpool sucks us in and we swim in never-ending circles of money-health-neighbors or children-work-husbands or clothes-travel-parties.

With others, worse yet. There is no whirlpool. Instead, we float like dry leaves on a still pond, touching only at the edges, if at all, until we drift away.

Recently my husband, Jack, and I spent four hours with friends we hadn't seen in years. My one attempt to find out what was really happening in their lives met with resistance. So we had a lovely meal, pleasant words, and a casual hug before we parted. Inside I was sick. The shallowness grieved me, in part because they wanted it that way.

But I have some friends who *never* talk trivia. The minute we get together, we plunge into the deep well of refreshing, stimulating conversation—usually about what God is doing in our lives or about things we are struggling with.

What a joy to be with them. I look forward eagerly to our times together. Those friends have become to me "fountains of life." They refresh my spirit, challenge my thinking, and glorify God.

The difference in these friends is in their hearts. God tells us, "Out of the abundance of the heart the mouth speaks" (Matthew 12:34, NKJ). When our minds dwell on surface issues, we talk of surface issues. When our thoughts are mostly on problems, clothes, jobs, or other daily concerns, that's what we talk about. When we dwell deep with God, we will be—to some people sometimes—a fountain of life.

Oh, don't let me intimidate you. Of course there is a place for small talk. Of course we'll discuss news and football games and our latest vacation. But is that all we talk about?

Proverbs 10:20 reproves me often: "When a good man speaks, he is worth listening to, but the words of fools are a dime a dozen" (TLB). Am I worth listening to? Or are my words a dime a dozen?

God spells out for us that which will make us worth listening to: "Talk with each other much about the Lord." Then He gives us some ideas on how to do that: "Quoting psalms and hymns and singing sacred songs, making music in your hearts to the Lord" (Ephesians 5:19, TLB). I love it! Can you remember ever saying, or having someone say to you, "Let's quote a psalm together" or "Let me share a hymn I've just memorized"? Even so, there are ways we can make music in our hearts to the Lord.

But how? Why? When? What?

I am convinced that if we dwell deep with God, the overflow is going to consistently seep into our conversations.

Jack and I were going through some painful things. Our future, in terms of his job situation, was vague. God kept our hearts full of peace and joy most of that time, but every once in a while we became disheartened.

One morning after a particularly discouraging Tuesday, Jack was headed upstairs and I was headed down when, almost in passing, I mentioned something God had spoken to me about in my time with Him. Then Jack said, "God has really been directing my heart to Psalm 62:5. It talks about putting my *expectations* in God alone. He seems to be saying to me that I can't expect any person to solve this situation. God is going to do it, and I need to expect nothing, except from Him."

Jack sat down on a stair and I perched on a lower one as we took five minutes together. Encouraging? You bet. That conversation was an overflow of Jack's life and walk with God.

How can we be people worth listening to?

By letting our lives be filled with God Himself. It's easy to write those words but difficult to do them. And, of course, it is *impossible* without God. He cannot be the "God out there" for you. He wants and needs to be the God *in* you, a Person who claims a vital, deep, consuming place in your life.

When he was twelve, my husband came into a relationship with Christ, as a result of a fight with the pastor's son. David and Jack were pummeling each other in the yard of the parsonage, dirt and fists flying, when Jack heard an authoritative voice say, "Stop that! Jack, come in here."

Jack thought, *Oh, boy, I'm going to get it now!* as he entered the pastor's study.

But instead of bawling Jack out, the pastor said, "Jack, have you ever asked Christ to come into your life?"

Jack had been in church services several times each week since he was five years old, but no one had ever asked him that question. He knew that he didn't live up to God's standards of righteousness—and that he never could. (How could he argue with that when he had just been caught fighting with the pastor's son?) Jack had been told that

Christ chose to die—a very cruel death on the cross—to pay the penalty for the sins of the world, even though He was sinless. The One who did no wrong became the substitute for the ones who deserved death and separation from God because of their sin. Jack understood that Christ died because He loved us, and this was the *only way* that mankind could ever be forgiven and enter into God's presence— both here on earth as well as in Heaven.

Yes, Jack knew all the facts. He just hadn't ever done anything about responding to those truths. He told the pastor, "No, I never have," and the pastor asked him if he would like to. When he answered, "Yes," the two of them knelt. Jack pressed his face into an old leather chair and invited the Lord Jesus Christ to come into his life to be his Savior. That day Jack became a child of God. His name was written in the Book of Life. He became a Christ-one.

The first step in letting God fill your life is inviting Him, in the Person of Christ, to come into your life. But some invite Him in and relegate Him to a corner of their heart. In order to have speech controlled by God, we must have *lives* controlled by God. He must fill us *full*.

The *how* of being people worth listening to is by letting our lives be filled with God Himself.

The *why* of being people worth listening to is because we are His, and He wants us to radiate Him.

When? Continually.

What should we talk about? Besides speaking of the Lord Himself, the list from Scripture includes the following.

Praise. "And I will tell everyone how great and good you are; I will praise you all day long" (Psalm 35:28, TLB). If we could put all our words for one week in a computer and have them analyzed to give us the average daily percentage of praise, what would it be? I have a feeling that rather than all day long, it would be more like two minutes.

I talked to a friend whose son-in-law had fallen 60 feet while rock climbing. He landed on his head and face, resulting in the loss of some vision and memory, and requiring multiple surgeries and months in rehabilitation. My friend said, "We praise God he is not paralyzed. He can walk and has frontal vision in one eye." Many of us would have enumerated the problems. My friend thanked God for the positives.

Greeting the day with praise to the Lord will help our thoughts and speech be full of His praises during the day. But often, as we talk on the telephone or chat with friends over coffee, our conversations are on what life has thrown at us instead of the things God is doing in our lives.

The Word of God. "These commandments that I give you today are to be upon your hearts. Impress them on your children. Talk about them when you sit at home and when you walk along the road, when you lie down and when you get up" (Deuteronomy 6:6-7).

I had lunch recently with a person who is new to Colorado Springs. Her depth of character is evident. As we talked of lessons God is in the process of teaching us, I told her of several enigmas in my life. She listened, then said thoughtfully, "Until recently, in a number of situations, I would think things like, *Well, if God doesn't provide the money for that couple to go to her sister's wedding, I'll give it to them.* Then it struck me that I was thinking that I am kinder than God. I'd be nicer if I were in control."

She drew my attention to Deuteronomy 32:4: "He is the Rock, his works are perfect, and all his ways are just. A faithful God who does no wrong, upright and just is he."

As I read this verse again and again, God worked in my life. I had been reading it something like this: "Most of the time, He is the Rock. His works are usually perfect, and a great deal of the time His ways are right. A faithful God who, when He chooses to get involved, does no wrong. At such times He is upright and just."

No! He is *always* the Rock. He is *always* in control. He is *always* faithful, involved, just, perfect.

In sharing the Word that afternoon, Jean hammered the final stroke to nail the lid down on a lesson God was fashioning for me. Jean had encouraged me through the Word of God.

Encouragement and comfort. I love Paul's reminder to the Thessalonians when he said, "For you know that we dealt with each of you as a father deals with his own children, encouraging, comforting and urging you to live lives worthy of God, who calls you into his kingdom and glory" (1 Thessalonians 2:11-12).

Even as I was writing those words, the doorbell rang, and I found the small daughter of a friend standing on the steps holding a plastic bag with four homemade cinnamon rolls in it. A couple of days before, my friend and I had taken her children to the zoo. A note was enclosed with the rolls quoting her oldest son, who said, "The nice thing about Mrs. Mayhall is that she seems to be always smiling." After a morning cleaning the garage, going to the doctor, and doing piles of laundry, that note made my day! Encouragement came when it counted.

How vital are words! Yet how often we fail to encourage, comfort, and urge people to "live lives worthy of God."

I recently had the privilege of spending a day with a well-known author. As I observed her life, I realized that either she had a natural gift of encouragement or had developed and honed it through the years. After asking some insightful questions of a young mother with three small children, the woman said, "Oh, you are so creative! Imagine thinking of things like that to tell them." (This from a woman who had written a book on training children). To a homemaker she commented, "What a tremendous idea! May I copy that from you?" To a workshop leader, she enthused, "I took five pages of notes in your workshop! Thank you for all that great material."

Words of encouragement and praise came naturally to her. She wasn't "putting it on." When I asked her if this encouragement was a gift or if she had developed it as a habit, she said both her father and her husband were natural encouragers and she probably "just picked it up."

Some of us need more help than others in developing the ability to be true encouragers. At one point in my life I asked the creative God for some creative ideas as to *how* to be an encourager. For some weeks I asked Him to put someone on my heart to specially encourage that day. It was fascinating to see the various ones He brought to my mind—the leader of our Bible study, the neighbor who was there in time of need, the accompanist at church. (Who ever writes the piano player a note of thanks or encouragement? If we compliment anyone at all, it is the soloist.)

One Thanksgiving, Jack received a long-distance phone call. The caller, a man, said, "In listing things and people for which I'm thankful, I realized that you probably didn't know that I came to Christ during a meeting at which you spoke many years ago. This Thanksgiving, I wanted to call you and thank you." What an encouragement!

Are you praying about developing the habit of encouragement? Are you asking a creative God for creative ideas in order to do this? It may mean a separate prayer list for you. It may take a page in your "do-list" notebook. But if your desire is to encourage, God will give you the ideas and the ability to grow to be a comforter and an encourager.

Wisdom and justice. "The mouth of the righteous man utters wisdom, and his tongue speaks what is just" (Psalm 37:30). How tremendous it would be if we processed everything we said through the list of characteristics in James 3:17. Are our words pure, gentle, peaceable, full of mercy and good fruit, unwavering, without hypocrisy? What a shining, joyful place this world would be if our words measured up to these attributes.

This is a partial list of what should proceed from our mouths, but perhaps it will give us a start in our thinking.

We need to marry two concepts and never divorce them. Ephesians 4:15 refers to "speaking the truth in love," and Proverbs 3:3 (TLB) says, "Never forget to be truthful and kind. Hold these virtues tightly. Write them deep within your heart."

Love, or kindness, and truth must be inseparable. Unfortunately, at times we think we are being loving by not speaking the truth. At other times we speak the truth, but are unloving as we do so. I wish I could place love and truth deep in my mind to filter every word I speak. Much would be left unsaid if these two concepts were the strainer used to purify my speech.

The wisest king of all, Solomon, said it well: "The words of the wise are like goads, their collected sayings like firmly embedded nails—given by one Shepherd" (Ecclesiastes 12:11).

Oh, that we will realize the power of our words—both for good and bad: "The tongue has the power of life and death" (Proverbs 18:21). If our tongues can be controlled, our mouths will be fountains of life, and we *will* be worth listening to.

BIBLE STUDY APPLICATION
1. a. Write Proverbs 10:11 in your own words.
   b. What does "fountain of life" mean?
   c. Think back over your conversations of the last week. What word or words describe your speech?

2. Have you participated in many or few significant conversations within the last month? What were the subjects of the meaningful times? With whom did you have these?

3. Write Proverbs 10:20 as a prayer. Then spend a few minutes talking and listening to God about your speech.

4. According to the following verses, what should be consciously woven into our conversations?
   a. Deuteronomy 6:6-9
   b. Proverbs 12:25
   c. Psalm 37:30-31
   d. Psalm 40:3

5. In a concordance find four more verses about speech. (Look up *tongue* or *mouth* or *speak.*) Write a paragraph about what God is saying and describe what action you should take *this week.*

"Aren't I Terrific?"

ON BRAGGING

It has happened at least three times in the last two weeks. And in one case, I was the culprit.

Scene one: I answered the doorbell's insistent ring to discover a well-dressed gentleman standing there with a package intended for my next-door neighbor, who is in the repair business. "I can't raise George," he said, "and I need this repaired before I leave for Denver later this afternoon."

Trying to be helpful, I said, "Well, sometimes he can't hear the doorbell over the noise of his machines."

"Then would you mind if I use your phone to see if he's there?" he questioned.

In the brief time of walking to the phone in the kitchen

and returning to the front door, I learned that he was to meet the president of a local bank for lunch, they were eating at an exclusive club in town, and he was a very busy man whose time was too important to waste getting something repaired. I blinked as he vanished, and thought to myself, *Now why did he tell me all of that?*

Scene two: I met a Christian speaker at the Denver airport, and we chatted for five minutes. In that time I was told the number of people to which she spoke (150), how many received Christ, and how God had blessed in every way.

Scene three: As a friend and I were leaving a restaurant, the hostess invited us to put our business cards into a bowl for a drawing for a free lunch. "I don't have any business cards," I replied. The hostess said that she was going to have some made for her second job, sales manager of a local company.

I said, "Well, I guess I could have some made that say 'Writer' or something." This, of course, forced the hostess to ask what I wrote. I guess that made me feel more like a somebody. But why did I say anything? It was totally unnecessary.

Name-dropping. Place-dropping. Event-dropping. Even successful-ministry-dropping. Oh, we wouldn't admit it, especially to ourselves. We'd say it was sharing answers to prayer or giving cause for rejoicing, *and it may be.* Only God can judge our motives. Yet Scripture tells us, "Let another praise you, and not your own mouth; someone else, and not your own lips" (Proverbs 27:2).

Good, sweet water and salty, poisoned water cannot come from the same well. But many of us try the impossible when it comes to words. The Apostle James says clearly, "With the tongue we praise our Lord and Father, and with it we curse men, who have been made in God's likeness. Out of the same mouth come praise and cursing. My brothers, this should not be. Can both fresh water and salt water flow from the same spring?" (James 3:9-11).

One way we continually contaminate the well of speech is by bragging or boasting. Most of us are adept at both in subtle and not-so-subtle ways. I often do one or the other without conscious thought. One morning Jack and I attended a prayer breakfast for our city. I planned to leave fifteen minutes before it concluded to get to a speaking engagement. I decided to slip to the back of the large room before the speaker started and listen from there so I wouldn't disturb anyone when I left. I explained this to the table hostess by saying, "I'm going to go to the back because I have to leave early for a speaking engagement."

True. But why didn't I merely say, "Please excuse me. I have to leave a bit early for an appointment"?

Obviously, we mustn't become overly concerned about this. Many times we want to, and should, share things with friends. And simply because we are human, we will tell things from our point of view. But the difference between sharing information and boasting is in *who gets the glory.*

Two people shared similar ministry experiences. One said, "God really used me. I led three people to Christ, and many others commented on how my message helped them." The other said, "As a result of your prayers, God worked in a wonderful way. Two people received Christ, and many expressed that they were touched by His hand."

In the first instance, our attention is focused on the speaker. In the second, it is focused on God. "It is not good to eat much honey, nor is it glory to search out one's own glory" (Proverbs 25:27, NASB). You see, when we seek out our own glory, we are usurping the glory of God.

Name-, place-, and event-dropping are boasting, and boasting is often on lists of characteristics of godless people in the Bible. Boasting is straight from a world that is going to pass away (see 1 John 2:16-17).

God's definition of boasting and my definition are a universe apart. I think of someone as bragging when he says or means, "Man, I'm a really talented guy." According to God's Word, it is bragging when we say, "I'm going to Denver next week." Hard to believe, isn't it? But the Book of James includes a helpful explanation:

> Now listen, you who say, "Today or tomorrow we will go to this or that city, spend a year there, carry on business and make money." Why, you do not even know what will happen tomorrow. . . . Instead, you ought to say, "If it is the Lord's will, we will live and do this or that." As it is, you boast and brag. All such boasting is evil. (James 4:13-16)

The word translated *brag* in verse 16 literally means a "wandering quack." A braggart boasts about things that he can't control and promises more than he can deliver.

Now what is this driving at, and why is it boasting? When I say I'm going to Denver next week, I'm implying that I'm in total control of what I do or don't do. And *that isn't true.* A cold breath from God can bring the city to a standstill under three feet of snow. Or, I may have to take care of my sick husband.

I do not have control over my life. My *times* and *timing* are in God's hand (see Psalm 31:15).

Of course you and I aren't going to go around tacking on the phrases *if God allows* or *if God wills* to every sentence of intent. But is that the *attitude of our heart?* Do we say, "I'm going to go to the conference this weekend" while in our heart we hold those plans up to the will and control of the Father? Somehow I doubt that most of us even think about that. Certainly, we have been unaware that we have been boasting. Perhaps we need to examine our heart—to pray, "Search me, O God, and know my heart" (Psalm 139:23) concerning boasting—not if we do, but to what degree. Then we must ask God for His healing light to be beamed on it, exposing it and cleansing it from our life and speech.

When we boast and brag about ourself, our accomplishments, our importance, or our status, we are not only committing a sin of *commission*, but two of *omission*. Bragging draws attention to the "I" of pr-I-de, which is a sin of commission. But we are also failing to give God the glory and failing to edify, or build up, other believers.

In studying Ephesians 4, I was struck by the fact that we are to build up or edify, not ourself, but our fellow Christians. My inevitable question as the Lord spoke gently to my heart was, "Yes, Lord. I want to do that. But please tell me how." As He often does, God quietly said, "I've already told you." As I restudied the chapter, I discovered God's instructions. He says the key to edifying others lies in who I *am* and in how I *speak*. So I wrote,

I am to *be*
      completely humble and gentle,
      patient,
      forbearing,
      in unity with one another,
      peaceful,
      sharing whatever gift I have with others,
      mature,
      and hardworking.
I am to *speak*
      the truth in love (never lie),
      without sinning in anger,
      quickly, to work through conflict,
      wholesome words,

that which is profitable,
with no bitterness, rage, anger, slander, or malice,
kindly,
compassionately (with understanding),
and with forgiveness.

As I stared at what I'd written, I thought, *This is a lifetime project!* It became very clear that boasting or bragging cannot coexist with being the kind of person who will edify others. I desperately need God's help in this, first, in making me sensitive to areas of boasting, and then, in helping me change those areas. But God *has promised* His help.

A little boy was trying to move a huge rock. He pulled and pushed, and tried to move it with leverage from a board. All to no avail.

His dad asked him, "Son, have you used all your resources?"

The son answered, "Yes, Dad. I've tried everything and I can't make it move."

His father replied, "No, you haven't. You haven't asked me to help you yet."

The Holy Spirit enables! He is our resource. He alone enables the light to shine through us—to help us in what we are and what we say so that we can edify other believers. He alone can make the poisoned well of our speech pure—free of boasting.

BIBLE STUDY APPLICATION

1. Read James 3 aloud, in a meditative way. Write down your observations concerning the tongue.
2. a. Write Proverbs 25:27 in your own words.
   b. In what ways do people try to gain glory for themselves?

   c. In what ways do you try to look important?
3. Read Ephesians 4:29-32. Describe the kind of talk that should come out of your mouth.
4. Compare Proverbs 27:2 with Philippians 2:3. Write a brief paragraph about your comparison as it relates to bragging versus humility.
5. Everyday for a week jot down the things that you said that could have been bragging. At the end of the week, pray about your list and ask God to make you conscious when you are being critical or trying to make an impression on others.

"Woe Is Me!"

ON COMPLAINING

Jack came out of the drugstore in Granby, Colorado, laughing. He had just seen a sign below a display for bug spray. The sign said, "BE A BELIEVER. THEY ARE COMING." Someone had scratched a line through the last three words and written instead, "They are here. And they are feasting." And feast they did that week, in spite of the bug spray Jack had purchased.

Words can be just as pesky—and cause a great deal more grief—than those gnats and mosquitos. And the pest that bites us often and causes huge welts to the skin of our soul—and the souls of those around us—is the pernicious habit of complaining.

A great many Christians, at times, are internal and infernal *gripers* (hopefully, not eternal, but sometimes it would seem so!). We complain. We criticize. We grouse, grouch, and grumble. The truth is, we are *contentious.*

Often we put a "but" at the end of a "thank you," as in, "Thank you, Lord, for friends, *but* I wish I had more;" or, "I'm grateful for my health, *but* I wish I weren't getting gray and creaky;" or, "I'm grateful for our home, *but* I wish we could afford new carpeting."

The story is told of a grandmother who was walking with her grandson along the beach. Suddenly a giant wave swept him away. The grandmother fell on her knees and prayed for his return. Another wave deposited him beside her. Astonished, she looked him over. He seemed to be all right. Then she noticed something and prayed, "Thank you for saving his life, *but* when we came, he had a hat!"

Perhaps the greatest reason for a complaining spirit is lack of contentment—with ourselves, with our situations, with our relationships, with the world in general. Because we are not *content*, we become *contentious.*

Our lack of contentment is often caused by our tendency to compare.

We start early. The eight-year-old adopted daughter of a friend of mine compared herself to her brother by saying, "He's home-grown and I'm store-bought."

And we keep doing it all our life. When we are not feeling good about ourselves, it is easy to find someone to compare ourselves to in a positive light. However, I am more prone to compare myself negatively.

Years ago I got caught up in the excruciating process of trying to be the perfect Christian worker's wife. I wanted to be hospitable like Marion, be the organizer and housekeeper that Lucy is, have the speaking ability of Leila, possess the gift of counseling that Morina has, and be the gentle lady that Helen is (and on and on). Somehow, I was always failing!

Then God said firmly to my heart, "Carole, who is the person you are trying to emulate?" So I started to enumerate. Only then did I realize I was trying to be a composite of about ten women. I'd painted all their best characteristics into my ideal picture and was killing myself trying to be all those at once.

I got the point. God wants me to be *me*. Sure, He has a lot of rough edges to file away, but He created only one me in the whole world, and I need to be *content* to be that.

Comparison rarely helps, and it's not scriptural. God's Word teaches that we are not wise to compare ourselves either negatively or positively: "We do not dare to classify or compare ourselves with some who commend themselves. When they measure themselves by themselves and compare themselves with themselves, they are not wise," or "are without understanding" (2 Corinthians 10:12, NASB). When we compare ourselves with others, we have neither understanding nor wisdom. Rather, "in humility consider others better than yourselves" (Philippians 2:3).

Our contentment—or lack of it—is often influenced by what we allow to come into our minds. If we are concerned about our speech, we must be careful what we *pour into* our minds. Reading romantic novels, even Christian ones, could bring despairing thoughts of how our husbands don't measure up to the heroes in those stories. I love good romances, but if I ever find myself starting to compare my husband negatively, they will have to go.

Have you ever bought a book and realized by the end of the first chapter that it is junk? Do you throw it into the garbage can or do you rationalize that you'll read it anyway so you won't waste your money? Friend, you've already wasted the money. The question is, are you going to waste hours on it, too, and in the process dump garbage into the well of your mind? "A wise man is hungry for truth, while the mocker feeds on trash" (Proverbs 15:14, TLB).

We must also be careful about what we allow to stay in our minds. Many people in our society today wrestle with unbelievable difficulties that cling to their lives like bloodsuckers. They have been victims of emotional or physical abuse, had marriages full of pain and anger, and have been violated, humiliated, and torn apart inside.

How they respond to these hurts varies greatly. Some are able, with the help of Christ, to forget those things that are behind them (Philippians 3:13). Others seem unable or unwilling to let the hurts go. They continually relive the ugly situations over and over in their minds. Consequently, they do not think about "whatever is lovely" (Philippians 4:8). They keep reloading into their minds thoughts from a tragic past, and live in depression and despair as they are haunted by those thoughts.

Being careful not to dump trash into our minds and not to allow ugliness from the past to stay there is only the first step. We may get rid of some of the poison, but if fresh, pure water is not constantly coming in, our well becomes stagnant and foul.

The Lord Jesus said to His disciples, "You are already clean *because of the word* I have spoken to you" (John 15:3, italics mine). The cleansing power of the Word of God cannot be over emphasized. When we stand near a bonfire, we come away smelling like smoke. When we walk through the world, we cannot help being contaminated in thoughts, in habits, in speech. We need—desperately need—the daily cleansing of God's Word, a time alone with Him each day, as well as special seasons of deeply searching for His truths.

I would challenge you to look up three things in Scripture tomorrow morning for which to thank the Lord. Then add three things from the world around you. Each morning add one more from both the Word and blessings God has given you. Then ask God to help you come back to those things and thank Him throughout the day. Do this for one month. Also memorize Ephesians 3:14-20 and direct your thoughts back to that passage every time your mind is free. My hope would be that after a month, you will have learned some new thought patterns that will take over for the rest of your life.

The Apostle Paul said, "I have learned to be content whatever the circumstances. I know what it is to be in need, and I know what it is to have plenty. I have learned the secret of being content in any and every situation, whether well fed or hungry, whether living in plenty or in want" (Philippians 4:11-12).

Dear friends, let's put that verse in context. It is preceeded by *commands* to rejoice, to be free from worry, to pray, to think about all the wonderful positives of Christ and His Word. And it is followed by a verse that tells us beyond a doubt that the ability to be content is given us through the power of Christ, who gives us the strength *to be content.*

That says a great deal to me. If I really am content with who I am, with what I have, and with the situations and world around me—if I can snuggle deep into the arms of a loving God and know with overwhelming gratitude that He loves me and cares for me—how can I complain?

Paul said he *learned* contentment. He didn't say he prayed for it, though he may have prayed that God would help him fulfill his responsibility to be content. Paul learned contentment, apparently by *experiencing* it, because he said, "I know what it is to be in need."

One of the fears of my life is that I won't learn through experience. Someone said, "Some people have twenty years of experience. Others have one year of experience repeated twenty times." They refuse to learn from experience.

I have been through times of want—times when we didn't know where the money was coming from for the next meal, let alone the month's rent. But have I learned contentment in this situation?

I have seen times of plenty—times of not being concerned if I spent an extra $10.00 at the grocery store. But have I learned contentment?

I long to live each day to the fullest—to squeeze from each moment every drop of joy, gladness, beauty, wonder, bewilderment, learning, even suffering if that is what the minute holds. But I can never live life to the hilt without learning to be *content* with the now.

We are told by Solomon, "It is better to live in a corner of the housetop than in a house shared with a contentious woman" (Proverbs 21:9, RSV). He went on to say, "A continual dripping on a rainy day and a contentious woman are alike; to restrain her is to restrain the wind or to grasp oil in his right hand" (Proverbs 27:15-16, RSV).

But lest we think women are the only ones at fault, a clear command is given to all believers in Philippians 2:14-16:

> Do everything without complaining or arguing, so that you may become blameless and pure, children of God without fault in a crooked and depraved generation, in which you shine like stars in the universe as you hold out the word of life.

Someone has said, "It is the look that saves, but the gaze that sanctifies." We look to the Savior for our salvation. But we must gaze intently at the Lord through the pages of His Word in order to purify and sanctify our life and our speech. When we drink deeply from the delights of His promises, slowly yet steadily, our contentiousness will turn to contentment, and our complaints to songs of praise.

BIBLE STUDY APPLICATION

1. Use a dictionary to define the words *contentment* and *complaint*.
2. Read Philippians 4:10-12, 1 Timothy 6:6-8, and Hebrews 13:5-6. List several observations about contentment.
3. a. In your own words, write Philippians 2:14-16.
   b. In what areas do you find yourself grumbling and complaining?
   c. Are there patterns to your complaints, such as the time of day, increasing pressures, or certain people?
4. a. Use Psalm 139:23-24 as a prayer, asking God for specific insight into when and why you complain and are not content.
   b. Write down one or two insights that God seems to be pointing out to you.
   c. Pray for wisdom. Then write down two things that you can do this week to stop complaining.
5. What do you feel is the key to contentment and godliness? See 2 Timothy 2:15 and 3:16-17.

⧼ 4 ⧽
"Don't Give It a Thought!"
ON RECKLESS AND CARELESS SPEECH

One of the dirtiest, greasiest, ugliest jobs around the house has to be cleaning the barbecue grill. With teeth clenched and perspiration dropping off my nose, I was working grimly at this task. Company was coming for hamburgers the next evening, and I knew that if I didn't get some of the grease off the grill, we could have burned hamburgers at best and a fire at worst.

In the middle of the task, I went inside to get some paper towels. Jack, who was trying hard to get back into a regular exercise program, was resting with his feet up on an ottoman.

"I've walked five miles today," he told me.

Without a thought, I said, "Boy, just think of all you could have accomplished with that kind of energy."

The minute I said it, I wanted to reach out and pull the words back. The joy of accomplishment drained from Jack's face. As I went to the basement, God convicted me of words that were both careless and hurtful.

Going back upstairs, I apologized profusely, and Jack said he forgave me. But the words had been said. I could not undo that. I remembered then the verse that says, "He who guards his lips guards his soul, but he who speaks rashly will come to ruin" (Proverbs 13:3).

Careless words are the result of not thinking before we speak. And many times they *hurt*.

"May I talk to you for five minutes?" Her lined, sweet face was distressed. Behind rimless glasses, her eyes glistened with tears. We stepped to one corner of the crowded conference room.

"Two years ago," she began, "after some physical problems and deep hurts in my life, I was on the verge of a nervous breakdown. I cried often and had to stop doing some jobs around the church. Then my minister visited me. He said, 'Unless you pull yourself together and snap out of this, the people in the church are going to stop praying for you.'"

Her tears welled up and overflowed as the memory of his remark made the wound break open and bleed once more. "I became so depressed after that, I did have a breakdown, and I've been two years recovering."

I cried with her. The minister's words had devastated her. Nevertheless, God used that experience in her life. After recovering, she became an empathetic visitor to many hospital patients. The week she talked to me, one had come to Christ. But the fact that God will use even the most ugly experience to train and mold a person doesn't relieve us as individuals of the responsibility of being careful—full of care—in what we say to a person.

Every time I read a verse about carelessness in speech, I am convicted. "Reckless words pierce like a sword," Proverbs tells us, "but the tongue of the wise brings healing" (12:18). In *The Living Bible,* the paraphrase of that verse reads, "Some people like to make cutting remarks, but the words of the wise soothe and heal."

The word *reckless* is defined as "careless, heedless, *not regarding consequences;* headlong and irresponsible; rash."[1] Some synonyms are incautious, unmindful, neglectful, unthinking, and thoughtless.

Making statements—and asking questions—without thinking can cause pain.

My sister, Joye, was dying of leukemia. Her beautiful blonde hair fell prey to extensive chemotherapy. Weight loss and the ravages of cancer both aged and grayed her parched skin. A newspaper clipping of her daughter's wedding was taped to the locker in her hospital room. A young student nurse breezed in, looked at the picture, and thoughtlessly said, "Oh, what a nice picture. Is that your granddaughter?" Tears formed beneath lashes of the one who had been taken as a sister to her daughter a year earlier.

I am convinced that *daily,* perhaps *hourly,* we need to ask God to help us bite our tongue before voicing careless remarks that can hurt, even devastate. We need to ask Him to help us *think* before we speak.

Often we are irresponsible and careless about *exaggeration.* In his book, *Tongue in Check,* Joseph Stowell writes, "Exaggeration is nothing more than lying about details to make information more sensational, interesting, or manipulative."[2] "Exaggeration erodes trust and credibility, two building blocks of successful relationships."[3]

When I read that, I winced. Hard. Jack sometimes teases me about exaggeration. He calls it a "writer's prerogative." But I have to face the hard fact that if I exaggerate deliberately with an intent to be sensational, interesting, or manipulative, it is *wrong*. I don't appreciate it in others, so I can't be soft on myself.

When I was growing up, members of my family sometimes deliberately overstated things to get a good argument going. A habit was grooved into my life long before I was married. I have needed the example of my husband, who rarely exaggerates or overstates. He tries to tell the facts—exactly.

We may also be careless when it comes to *flattery*. To flatter means to praise too much, untruthfully, or insincerely in order to win favor. When we flatter, we may be trying to place someone in debt to us by commending an action, an ability, or a physical or character trait. It differs from genuine praise or compliment by its motive.

It is possible for the same words to be a sincere compliment for encouragement or to be insincere flattery for manipulation or personal gain. I could say to my husband, "I so appreciate your consideration and thoughtfulness" out of honest appreciation for those qualities or in the hope of getting something I want.

In order to know my motives, I have to be sensitive to the still small voice of the Holy Spirit when He taps me on the shoulder and says, "Carole, watch it!"

The carelessness of our speech may also show up in our lack of wisdom when we spout surface answers to deep problems and hurts.

After my sister's painful death, I went through a period of non-feeling. I seemed to be dead inside—void of any feeling, either happy or sad. Even my times with the Lord were blah. When I told an acquaintance of this, she said quickly, "It must be an attack of Satan." It wasn't, but her surface answer stifled further discussion.

Before Joye's death, I could have given you several reasons for pain and suffering. After her death, I could have given you those same reasons. But I *wouldn't* have. I came to realize that reasons don't help when a person is crushed with grief.

I heard singer and composer John Fischer say, "Much of my life falls between the answers." Many of us experience this. Not that there aren't answers. But God's ways are higher than either our ways or our comprehension. In the complexities of life, we flounder until we accept the fact that while truth is simple, life is, in many cases, impossible to understand.

Please then, deliver me from clichés. Deliver me from pat answers. Deliver me from surface statements about deep and complex issues. Deliver me from careless speech.

But what, oh what, can we do about the times we see the tendency toward rash and careless speech in our own life?

First of all, we need to pray for quick sensitivity to the voice of the Holy Spirit. When He convicts us, we must confess our speech as sin. It is more than a goof, a slip of the tongue. It is *sin* that we must confess. We must also ask God's help to improve in this area.

That day I was cleaning the barbecue grill and hurt Jack with my waspish words, God showed me I was wallowing in self-pity for having to do such a dirty job, and in envy that Jack could put his feet up and rest. Well, what's wrong with that? Self-pity cannot coexist with a thankful spirit. Singing songs about "poor me" drowns out making melody in my heart to God.

Self-pity is far easier than self-control, especially because "self-control means controlling the tongue!" (Proverbs 13:3, TLB). Being human, I don't always have a great attitude or unlimited self-control. When I don't, I need God's "guard"—His control—not to speak rashly. But I also need to continue to work on changing my thought patterns.

The most practical method in my own life to change my thoughts has been to memorize Scripture and to ask God to help me *put into practice* truths such as, "A good man thinks before he speaks; the evil man pours out his evil words without a thought" (Proverbs 15:28, TLB). The *New International Version* says, "The heart of the righteous weighs its answers."

In addition, ask God for a faithful friend (a friend-husband is wonderful) who will bring to your attention those attitudes and words that grieve the Father-heart of God. Scripture encourages such help: "He who listens to a life-giving rebuke will be at home among the wise. He who ignores discipline despises himself, but whoever heeds correction gains understanding" (Proverbs 15:31-32).

Yes, it will hurt. It isn't fun to discover ugly tendencies. Somehow our old nature is always there to jump in and take over the moment we relax the guard over our lips. However, if we really mean business in obeying God, this area of our life must be put on the altar of sacrifice to Him. I am convinced that this is part of being "living sacrifices, holy and pleasing to God" (Romans 12:1).

NOTES

1. *Webster's New World Dictionary of the American Language,* Second College Edition (Cleveland, New York: William Collins & World Publishing Company, Inc., 1974), page 1186.

2. Joseph M. Stowell, *Tongue in Check* (Wheaton, Illinois: Victor Books, 1983), page 51.

3. Stowell, page 52.

BIBLE STUDY APPLICATION

1. What do the following verses say about our speech?

Proverbs 12:18
Proverbs 13:2-3
Matthew 12:35-36

2. Think of a time you were either tempted to or actually did exaggerate. What was the reason?

3. a. Read Proverbs 15:28 carefully. Then write it in your own words.

   b. In one sentence explain how you have failed to obey this verse.

   c. Give one specific illustration of not obeying.

   d. After praying about this verse, write down two things you could do to put it into practice this week.

   (Two things are always possible: You can put the verse at the top of your prayer list for one week, and you can memorize the verse, asking God to remind you of it everytime you are quick to speak. By adding one other step—looking at the verse in its context—you have a wonderful tool in studying the Word.)

5
"Aha!"

ON SLANDER AND GOSSIP

The coffee pot gave one last burp and subsided. Ann poured the hot liquid into brightly painted mugs and placed one before each of the women gathering for prayer. The conversation was lively.

"I just drove by Rhonda's house, and it's up for sale."

"Yes, I know. She and her husband have separated—another woman involved, I think."

"I've heard that, too. She's really got problems. Her son was with the gang that was arrested the other night."

"I've been concerned about her being so strict with her kids for some time. I knew they would rebel one day."

"Yes, she certainly needs our prayers."

We could all think back to similar conversations we've had with people who, thinking they were gathering for prayer, were actually engaged in slander. *Slander?* we gasp. Yes. Slander.

Usually we think of slander as a false statement made about someone with malicious intent. The dictionary backs this up by defining slander as "the utterance in the presence of another person of a false statement or statements, damaging to a third person's character or reputation: usually distinguished from *libel,* which is written."[1]

However, in the Bible, the definition of slander goes beyond making false statements. In the Old Testament the word *slander* was used for bad reports in general. The Hebrew word meaning "to defame or to strip one of his positive reputation"[2] was used in the account of Joseph's true but "bad report" to his father concerning the wickedness of his brothers (Genesis 37:2). The same word was used in Numbers 13:32, the account of the ten spies who brought back a negative report about the Promised Land.

In the New Testament, the word for slander is comprised of two words, one meaning "against" and the other meaning "to speak." A slanderer, then, is simply one who speaks against another: "Anyone who speaks against his brother or judges him speaks against the law and judges it" (James 4:11). Based on the Old and New Testaments, slander is the *open, intentional sharing of damaging information* and is characterized by bad reports that blemish or defame a person's reputation *whether they are true or not!*

In commenting on James 4:11 in *The Expositor's Bible,* Alfred Plummer writes:

> The context shows what kind of adverse speaking is meant. It is not so much abusive or calumnious [malicious] language that is condemned, as the *love of finding fault.* The

censorious temper is utterly unchristian. It means that we have been paying an amount of attention to the conduct of others which would have been better bestowed upon our own. It means also that we have been paying this attention, not in order to help, but in order to criticize, and criticize unfavorably. . . . But over and above all this, censoriousness is an invasion of the divine prerogatives. It is not merely a transgression of the royal law of love, but a setting oneself above the law, as if it were a mistake, or did not apply to oneself. It is climbing up on to that judgment-seat on which God alone has the right to sit, and a publishing of judgments upon others which He alone has the right to pronounce.[3]

Mr. Plummer refers to the law of *love,* which James mentions, and writes:

If with full knowledge of the royal law of charity, and with full experience of the vexation which adverse criticism causes, he still persists in framing and expressing unfriendly opinions respecting other people, then he is setting himself up as superior, not only to those whom he presumes to judge, but to the law itself. He is, by his conduct, condemning the law of love as a bad law, or at least as so defective that a superior person like himself may without a scruple disregard it.[4]

Those are hard words—convicting words. It never occurred to me that when I was criticizing, I was in a very real sense slandering, and thus setting myself above a law of God.

There are times, of course, that truth, however harsh, must be shared. But some guidelines as to with whom, how, and when are imperative.

With whom: Does the person need to know because of his involvement or his responsibility in the situation? If the answer is yes, then it may not be slander.

How: Your attitude is important. Are you sorry or glad to make this known? Is it painful for you to share it, or are you needlessly making someone else look bad? Have you spoken first to the person you will be talking about?

When: Only when it is imperative.

And of course, when in doubt, *don't*! Heed the warning of the Apostle James: "Brothers, do not slander one another" (James 4:11).

Fortunately, there is a positive side. God never leaves us without one. Our words, which proceed from our thoughts, are to be wholesome.

At the end of his second letter to "God's elect, strangers in the world," Peter tells the readers his purpose in writing: "I have written both of them as reminders to stimulate you to wholesome thinking" (2 Peter 3:1). Our thinking is to be moral, honorable, responsible, virtuous, innocent, exemplary—synonyms for *wholesome.* We are to think about those things that improve our mind and character.

God wants us to think about what is true, noble, right, pure, lovely, admirable, excellent, and praiseworthy (see Philippians 4:8).

This is quite a list! If we were to judge all our words, let alone our thoughts, on the basis of this list, how do you think we would come out? Remember, to God *our thoughts are words.*

Peter tells how to develop this wholesome thinking. He writes, "I want you to recall the words spoken in the past by the holy prophets and the command given by our Lord and Savior through your apostles" (2 Peter 3:2). In other words, as we recall the *Word of God,* as we meditate on the Word more and more, our thinking will be conformed to His and we will radiate Him. We will glorify Him. We will praise Him. We will exemplify wholesome thinking.

The rest of 2 Peter 3 is a treasure chest brimming over with precious stones, principles telling how to change negative thought patterns into right thinking. The first diamond is in verse 3: "First of all, you must *understand.*" How frequently do we pray for understanding? How much time do we give to ponder, to think about, to gain an understanding of the deep truths of Scripture? If we neglect this, we are disobeying God's command.

The next precious stone in the chain is in verse 8: "But *do not forget.*" When something happens to test our faith, how quickly we forget God's work in our life and all He has done for us in the past. We are told not to forget.

A great pearl is found in verse 14. We are to *"make every effort* to be found spotless, blameless and at peace with him." How lackadaisically we pursue holiness. We think it is something that should happen *to* us or perhaps *for* us, instead of determining to go after it, to pursue it with every fiber in our being.

The next glittering gem teaches that we are to *be on guard* (verse 17).

And the gold chain that links them all together is in verse 18: We are to grow in the grace and knowledge of our Lord and Savior Jesus Christ.

Notice the verbs: understand, remember, make every effort, be on guard, grow. All these actions are necessary if we are to think and speak what is right—if we are to be wholesome in our thinking.

It is a proven psychological fact, as well as a truth of Scripture, that we *are* what we *think.* What we think about is going to spill out in what we say. That's why our thoughts need to be wholesome so that our speech will become more pleasing to God.

When our thoughts are not lovely, one of the results in our speech is the ugliness of gossip. Someone has defined gossip as "acid indiscretion." A gossip separates close friends (see Proverbs 16:28). The Bible tells us what our response should be to a person who gossips: "A gossip betrays a confidence; so avoid a man who talks too much" (Proverbs 20:19). Did you ever avoid a person who gossips—who "talks too much"?

In Scripture, gossip is coupled with quarreling, jealousy, outbursts of anger, factions, arrogance, disorder, and every kind of wickedness (see Romans 1:29 and 2 Corinthians 12:20). We live in bad company when we gossip!

The Apostle Paul felt that young widows could easily get into the habit of being idle and going about from house to house. "And not only do they become idlers, but also gossips and busybodies, saying things they ought not to" (1 Timothy 5:13).

The opposite of a gossip is a *trustworthy* man. In Proverbs 11:13 we read, "A gossip betrays a confidence, but a trustworthy man keeps a secret." Do we want to be worthy of someone's trust? Of course! Yet we betray members of the family of God by passing on unkind things we've heard about them or experienced with them.

Our accusations—in thought and word—are commonly directed against our own family of God. But the Apostle Paul asks, "Who are you to criticize the servant of somebody else, especially when that somebody else is God? It is to his own master that he gives, or fails to give, satisfactory service. And don't doubt that satisfaction, for God is well able to transform men into servants who are satisfactory" (Romans 14:4, PH).

We admit criticism and gossip are wrong and we shouldn't do it. But how can we *stop?* Or when we are in the middle of a gossip session, how can we extract ourselves?

A primary rule is to *plan ahead.* When hostessing, control the direction of conversation instead of letting it drift where it may. I am often involved in salad luncheons, which we call "Prayer and Share" luncheons. Almost without exception, the hostess guides the conversations into channels that help us talk about what God is doing in our lives, and about prayer requests we have. Seldom have I come away from such a luncheon wishing I hadn't heard or said a particular thing.

Another rule to keep in mind, whatever the setting, is that *the absent one should be safe* among those who are present. Oh, that we could follow that rule in our churches and every other gathering of Christ-ones.

Our homes are an important place where we should *guard against gossip.* Frequently Jack and I talk over a coming dinner party, suggesting topics of conversation we think would be either fun or edifying.

And what if you are caught in the middle of a group that is tearing someone down? Recently in a Bible study, one woman who works constantly with professional women said, "When I find myself in a group that is tearing someone to shreds, I smile sweetly and say, 'You know, I'm getting very uncomfortable about this.'" When asked what the response usually was to her statement, she said, "They change the subject." What a gracious and gentle way to let a group know that you aren't condemning them for gossiping, but you don't want to continue with it either.

Another suggestion was to respond softly, "That would really hurt her if she knew what we were saying."

I should not fail to pray each morning of my life, "Set a guard over my mouth, O LORD; keep watch over the door of my lips" (Psalm 141:3). I must confess that I forget to pray this sometimes, and as a result, words come out of my mouth that dishonor God and hurt people.

Do you pray when the telephone rings, when you meet a friend for lunch, when a group gathers together? Do you ask God to guard what you say and make you sensitive to His voice of warning, of control? Do you pray to be kind instead of cruel, gentle instead of harsh, building up instead of tearing down?

My life, my words, my thoughts are not hidden from God. Psalm 139 tells me that God perceives my thoughts from afar. He knows every word I'm going to say *before* I say it. The darkness of heart and mind in which I think I'm hiding is brilliant sunlight to God.

We often take lightly as a "little sin" what God takes very seriously. Now please don't misunderstand me. All through the Bible, we see men who poured out their hearts to an understanding Father. Many emotions—despair, anger, frustration—were spilled out, spit out, cried out to God. The psalmists, especially, were utterly transparent— honest before an all-knowing Jehovah. There are times when we need to bring things before the Lord, too, in an honest outpouring of our pain, disappointment, yes, even our anger.

David spewed out his gripes, his grievances, his desire for God to avenge him. And as far as I've discovered, God never got angry or bawled out David or others for doing this. But overall, David's life and speech reflect praise, not vengeance. He radiated God's light more than he despaired of the darkness, and so did the other godly men and women of the Bible.

Slander begins in the mind. It is born in the sinful nature and nourished by relishing resentment and feeding envy. It grows until it erupts as a disfigured monster hiding under a mask of respectability.

Discipline can conquer that monster. In his book *The Power of Commitment,* Jerry White defines discipline as "the ability to say 'no' to what is sin, to say 'yes' to what is right, and to say 'I will' to what ought to be done."[5] Therefore, may we determine not to slander, determine to discipline our minds to wholesome thinking, and determine to obey God.

> Oh Father! I am feeling so ashamed right now. How I have grieved You with my thoughts and my words. Forgive me, please. And deliver me from slander—from tearing down a servant of Yours. Set a watch before my tongue. Keep the door of my lips, that I might *glorify* You. Amen.

NOTES

1. *Webster's New World Dictionary of the American Language*, Second College Edition (Cleveland, New York: William Collins & World Publishing Company, Inc., 1974), page 1337.
2. James Strong, *Strong's Exhaustive Concordance of the Bible* (New York: Abingdon Press, 1890), page 29 in the Hebrew and Chaldee Dictionary.
3. Alfred Plummer, *The Expositor's Bible*, ed. W. Robertson Nicoll (Grand Rapids, Michigan: Baker Book House, n.d.), page 251.
4. Plummer, page 253.
5. Jerry White, *The Power of Commitment* (Colorado Springs, Colorado: NavPress, 1985), page 74.

BIBLE STUDY APPLICATION

1. a. Define the words *slander* and *gossip*.
   b. What do you feel is the difference between sharing confidences and slandering someone?
2. What do the following verses teach about slander or gossip?
   a. Proverbs 11:13
   b. Proverbs 16:28
   c. Proverbs 20:19
   d. Proverbs 26:20
3. a. What sins are listed with slander and gossip in Romans 1:29 and 2 Corinthians 12:20?

    b. Do you mentally put these sins in one category and gossip and slander in another category?

    c. Where do you think God puts gossip and slander?

4. What commands about slander are given in James 4:11 and 1 Peter 2:1?

5. a. Paraphrase Romans 14:4.

    b. What are some ways we judge someone?

    c. Against whom do you frequently pass judgment?

    d. What do you feel God wants you to do about this?

⸎ 6 ⸎
"That Makes Me Mad!"
ON ANGER AND CONFLICT

Jack and I shoehorned ourselves into the booth and were deciding on breakfast when another couple entered the small coffee shop and took the booth behind us. There was a moment of silence as they looked over the menu. Then the man asked, "What are you going to have?"

Instantly the woman snapped, "Why do you always ask me what I'm going to have?"

The man responded heatedly, "Good night! What's the matter? Are you threatened or intimidated or something?"

She shot back, "You're really looking for a fight this morning, aren't you?"

Their voices rose with each exchange.

I couldn't believe it! How could two people start the day arguing over a simple question like, "What are you going to have?"

Fortunately, the couple realized how ridiculous the whole thing was, and the woman had the grace to laugh and begin the day in a better frame of speech.

People can argue about anything.

Jack and I were giving a little quiz at a marriage seminar to see how well the couples really knew each other. We intended for it to be a break in the schedule and—we hoped—enlightening as well as fun. We had asked three questions, one of them being, "What is your spouse's favorite color?" Suddenly we heard a man's angry voice at the back of the room: "For crying out loud. You don't know my favorite color?"

Many books—good ones, too—have been written on the subject of anger. I'm not going to try to explore the topic here. But I do want to speak to a couple of issues about anger that relate to our tongues.

The Bible says, "Everyone should be quick to listen, slow to speak and slow to become angry." Why? "For man's anger does not bring about the righteous life that God desires" (James 1:19-20). God wants us to live righteously, doing what is right—by God's standard, not ours. Our anger, God says, is not going to bring about the kind of righteous life He wants us to live.

In practice, I'm often slow to hear (one might say "hard of hearing"), quick to speak, and instantly angry. The latter is much more controlled at this point in my life, but the "quick to speak" is too frequent, even yet.

Let's look at a couple of the most obvious reasons we are quick to speak and get angry. Many times when I stop to examine why I'm feeling irritated, I discover it is because physically I'm tired or tense, or it's the difficult time of month; or emotionally my reserves are low; or spiritually I'm drained. The first step, then, is to keep in control while I *determine the cause.*

It happened at least twenty years ago, but I remember as though it were yesterday. The sun was shining that Sunday morning as I got up to prepare breakfast for Jack and Lynn in our small townhome. While they were seated at the table, I began to talk and the more I talked, the crabbier I got. I started, as far as I can remember, with a few remarks about how busy a morning it was, and ended by practically shouting at them, "Oh, you probably don't want to go to church with me anyhow! Why don't you just go back to bed?"

The whole time, they had not uttered a word! I turned to face them angrily. Both were wide-eyed and open-mouthed with surprise.

Their expressions were so funny, I started to laugh. "Erase everything I've said for the last five minutes. It's that time of month. Forgive me!" We all relaxed as I served breakfast and then spent needed extra time with the Lord.

You women who know which days of the month are difficult may need to take some action.

1. Mark your calendar to identify those days when you are likely to be under strain.

2. Several days ahead, begin to pray for extra strength, control, and calmness. I call this "preventive prayer." When you see very busy days ahead during times of known stress, ask a couple of friends to pray for you.

3. Plan something relaxing and fun during that time (lunch with a friend, a date for the symphony, or a bike ride). Maybe what you need is a good nap while your husband or a friend takes the children to the park.

For me, the emotional and spiritual are often related. When I am depleted spiritually, I become angry more quickly and either start a quarrel or enter one at the first provocation. When my walk with God is vital, somehow He keeps my emotional well-being stable. A time of drinking deeply from the river of His delights brings me joy and peace (see Psalm 36:8).

Another reason for anger is that we feel our rights have been violated. Sometimes I get discouraged with how much of *me* is in me! I want things my own way, in my time frame, at my pace, and at my convenience. But life usually isn't like that. And God won't let it be often because, if it were, I'd be utterly selfish and self-centered.

When I memorized Proverbs 13:10, the lessons bombarded me. It says, "Only by pride cometh contention" (KJV). I thought, *Wait a minute here! Can this possibly mean that whenever I feel contentious, upset, angry, it is due to pride? That's hard to swallow.* So I began to check all my angry feelings against this verse. Pride is an unduly high opinion of yourself; exaggerated self-esteem. It is putting yourself and what you are doing ahead of others and what they are doing.

When Lynn, age three, dragged in three friends with muddy feet over my freshly cleaned and waxed kitchen floor, I was annoyed with her. Why? She hadn't considered my hard work (pride of self). When Jack brought unexpected company home for dinner, I was indignant. Why? He hadn't considered the extra work it was for me.

It began to dawn on me that except for righteous indignation—anger about sin committed against someone else—my anger did indeed stem from putting me and my feelings first. (I'm not saying that those kinds of things should not be talked through and resolved, but the cause must be identified and if it is pride, confessed.)

This pride can spill over to include those I love. Because Jack and I are one in marriage, because Lynn and her husband, Tim, and our two grandchildren are part of our family, I get as fiercely protective of their feelings—or more so—

than I do my own. I get angry when someone I love is hurt.

I sat and listened, outwardly calm. Inwardly, I was in shock. The speaker was talking about his perception of Jack. And forming in my total being, pushing to the limits of heart and mind, screaming to get out, was one pulsating NO.

"You're wrong!" I screamed inwardly.

But I said nothing.

What do you do when you or one you love is maligned or rejected? What do you do when you see the hurt of defeat and failure in the eyes of that dear one, and it has been caused by people close to you? What do you do when you feel betrayed?

You rant and rave and scream—if you don't know that the end result is meant for *good* in your life.

When we are hurt deeply, it is time to stop and examine both the reason for the pain and the purpose of God in that pain. If it's meant for good; if the bottom line is that God has allowed it in His *kindness* (ugly and hurtful as the process may have been) to perfect and hone us to be more like Jesus and to prepare us for a more fruitful life and for eternity; if we believe that, then we will accept it with a pure heart and clear conscience and *without quarrel.*

We must control anger. We must accept the situation that caused it as from a God of love and compassion. And we must learn from it.

Anger is an emotion just as sadness, joy, and fear are emotions. Many people say that an emotion is neither good nor bad—it just *is.* I won't argue that point. It is, however, very clear in Scripture that the godly way to handle anger is with self-control: "In your anger do not sin" (Ephesians 4:26).

Oh, my friends, there will be no exception to this rule. When we scream, rant, get hysterical, say vicious things— *whenever* we lose control—we sin against God and man. One fruit of the Holy Spirit is *self*-control (see Galatians

5:22-23), control of our tongue, our emotions, the tone of voice we use, our facial expressions, and our actions.

During her married life, my mother's mother was ninety pounds of dynamite. She and my grandfather pioneered a ministry in a lawless mountain town of Colorado. Later, in a small town in northern Michigan, she remained uncowed when their only horse was shot as a warning for my grandfather to cease preaching against alcohol. Without flinching she braved a threatening note that unless he stopped, their only daughter would be kidnapped. In her early fifties, when my grandfather died, Grandmother moved into our home, and we became her life.

As she grew older, she deteriorated mentally. Many times around the supper table, our whole family would roar with laughter at something funny or just plain silly. Everyone, that is, except Grandmother. She would cock her head like some white-crested, thin-faced bird, and peer narrowly into each face. Her expression said, "Each of you is crazy."

There were times when our arguing (we *loved* to argue!) would be too much for Dad. Then he would bring his fist down on the table and say firmly, "That's enough!" But I can never remember him speaking an angry or unkind word to Grandmother. She must have tried his patience and exasperated him many times. But my father had self-control, and he remained kind and controlled toward Grandmother for the twenty some years she lived with us until one night, in her sleep, God took her to Heaven.

Scripture says, "Let your forbearing spirit be known to all men" (Philippians 4:5, NASB). My father had that forbearing spirit. He exemplified the godly characteristics of an elder or overseer, who "must be above reproach as God's steward, not self-willed, not quick-tempered, not addicted to wine, not pugnacious, not fond of sordid gain, but hospitable, loving what is good, sensible, just, devout, *self-controlled*" (Titus 1:7-8, NASB).

We probably all have a problem with self-control in some area. We observe young parents shouting and screaming at their small children, and remember that for the parents the days seem long and the nights short. We understand and empathize. We have all seen athletes lose control.

But what about you? What is your special nemesis, or downfall? Do you lose your temper when you've been cooped up with the kids all day and your husband plunks down to read before supper? Are you grouchy for three days when you don't get your way?

I know people who feel they are being "real" and "open" when they explode and tell someone off in no uncertain terms. Because they are being "honest," the explosion is justified as being all right.

No. It is all wrong. Yes, we need to be honest. Yes, we need to be open. Yes, we need to let others know what we are thinking. But not without being loving, kind, and in control.

Quarreling should *not* be a part of our life. Paul tells us, "And the Lord's servant must not quarrel; instead, he must be kind to everyone, able to teach, not resentful. Those who oppose him he must gently instruct, in the hope that God will grant them repentance leading them to a knowledge of the truth" (2 Timothy 2:24-25).

Quarreling indicates anger—a desire to win—negative emotions. As a servant of the Lord, I *must* not quarrel. Raised voices are not gentle. So when we get hot under the temper, we need to step aside to pray, cool off, and ask for wisdom.

When we have identified an area of poor self-control that sometimes breaks down in anger, we can take concrete steps to correct it. We can take it to God in special prayer. We can memorize verses on patience (the opposite of lack of control), and ask those who are close to us to monitor our reactions in specific situations.

Quarreling in anger and working through conflict are totally different matters. Working through conflict is part of iron sharpening iron, speaking the truth in love, not sinning in anger, building others up, and walking in the light (see Proverbs 27:17 and 1 John 1:7).

Conflict, and working through that conflict, may be an everyday occurrence. It is part of the process of gentle instruction referred to in 2 Timothy 2:25. Too many people sweep their anger into the dust bin when things have cooled. But the dust keeps getting thicker until love is choked to death. Later, we stir up instant quarrels when we are hurt because we are grappling with deep-seated rage from all that accumulated dirt—anger that we may not even be aware we are nourishing in the darkness.

We can *use* situations that produce anger to work through conflict in a constructive way. My husband generally arrives home from work about 6:00 p.m., and I try to have dinner ready close to that time. One evening years ago, when steak was a rarity because of an extremely tight budget, I splurged to fix Jack's favorite dinner—steak, a baked potato, and apple pie. I even set the table with candles and all the finery I could muster.

The steak was done at exactly 6 o'clock. But no Jack. 6:30 came. 7:00 p.m. By 7:30 the steaks were cold, and I was hot! I was not only angry, but worried. When Jack breezed in at 7:45 to tell me he'd gotten caught up in some Christmas shopping, I was furious! He had violated what Dr. James Dobson, a Christian psychologist, calls a person's "line of respect." His actions had seemingly demonstrated that he didn't care about my time, feelings, or the steak dinner I'd so painstakingly prepared.

I had a choice at this point. I could blow up in anger or use this situation to clarify what is acceptable behavior for mutual respect and consideration at our house. I did both, but the blow-up didn't help one bit.

Resolving conflict takes self-control. I may be emotional (I am an emotional person), but if I am out of control, I need to stop and back off until I regain control. Then I won't say destructive and unkind things I don't mean and shouldn't say. And I am able to remember some rules such as sticking to the subject, being wise in what I say, seeing the other person's side of things, and being willing to compromise and change. I have to come to a better understanding of the person and the situation, and then agree on a mutually constructive solution.

Some specific questions and guidelines may help us:

1. *Do I have valid cause for conflict?* What am I really angry about? Is it merely a bad mood due to something physical that will improve tomorrow? Could it be that I am thinking only of myself?

Might this conflict be a "stupid argument"? It would be wise for us to heed the warning Paul gave to Timothy: "Don't have anything to do with foolish and stupid arguments, because you know they produce quarrels. And the Lord's servant must not quarrel" (2 Timothy 2:23-24).

Perhaps half of our conflicts would stop if we paused to ask ourself, Is this a matter of consequence or stupidity? Any issue that cannot or will not be resolved may be a stupid argument (for example, different views on a doctrinal issue or one or both parties being unwilling to be reasonable). Some of us need grace to live at peace with all men even when we don't agree.

2. *Have both parties defined the conflict?* Does everyone clearly know what the issue is? Have we defined the conflict to the other's satisfaction?

Many times I've heard a wife say of her husband, "But he should *know* how I feel!" Women are especially good at believing their husbands should know and respond to their feelings, desires, and pains without telling them what those feelings, desires, and pains are in plain words. Many conflicts would dissolve if we would "speak the truth in love" by *expressing* what we need, how we feel, how we are interpreting their speech or actions.

For example, a wife might say to her husband, "The issue as I see it is priorities for your time. I feel it is important that at least one evening a week is spent with the children and me in quality time. To me, it doesn't look as though you think this is important because you keep letting everything interrupt or conflict with our family time. If I hear you right, you are saying the time should be so flexible that it can be made up later if something else comes up. Is that right?"

3. *Have I clearly stated what I want and need?* In the situation above, the wife might say, "I feel it is of vital importance both to me and the children to have this time with you when you are not distracted. To me that means taking the phone off the hook, or going out to eat. I want you to be involved in making plans to spend time together and in carrying out those plans. What's your reaction?"

4. *Talk and compromise until you come to a mutually agreed-upon solution.*

5. *Keep short accounts.* The Apostle Paul advises, "Do not let the sun go down while you are still angry, and do not give the devil a foothold" (Ephesians 4:26-27). Don't let more than twenty-four hours pass before resolving a conflict, even if it means coming back to it several times. In the event of a major disagreement, at least agree to discuss it at a specified time in the very near future.

Of course, we need enough time—a few minutes to a couple of hours sometimes—to be able to step back and look at the situation with understanding and perhaps even humor. I think many of us need to pray, "Lord, don't let me lose my ability to laugh—especially at myself."

Henry Ward Beecher, a nineteenth-century preacher, once quipped, "Speak when you are angry and you'll make the best speech you'll ever regret."[1]

Gradually, as a growing Christian—as a person-in-process—I should have less anger and more self-control in my life. One aspect of maturity is the ability to control anger, to work through differences of opinion, and to grow both in dealing with and working through conflict, thus exemplifying one fruit of the Spirit—self-control.

> I cling to your commands and follow them as closely as I can. Lord, don't let me make a mess of things. (Psalm 119:31, TLB)

NOTES

1. As quoted in *Tongue in Check*, by Joseph M. Stowell (Wheaton, Illinois: Victor Books, 1983), page 91.

BIBLE STUDY APPLICATION

1. What do the following verses teach concerning your anger?
   Psalm 4:4
   Proverbs 29:22
   Ecclesiastes 7:9
   1 Corinthians 13:4-5
2. What do the following verses teach concerning the anger of others?
   Proverbs 15:1
   Proverbs 22:24
3. a. What do you think it means to be "slow to become angry"?

  b. What caused you to be angry during the last two
     weeks?
  c. Were you quick or slow to anger?
  d. How could you work on this specifically? See Psalm
     131:2-3.
4. Memorize Colossians 3:8 or James 1:19-20. Then use
   this memorized Scripture to pray about someone with
   whom you are quick to get angry.

« 7 »

"Lord, Help Me to Think!"

ON DISCRETION

An elevator whooshed the boisterous group of laughing couples to the revolving restaurant high above the city. While waiting for coffee and dessert, we gazed at the lights far below us.

"Boy, this makes me a little dizzy," said one wife.

Without skipping a beat, her husband teased, "Honey, are you sure it's the height?"

Sometimes it's very discouraging giving marriage seminars! You see, Jack and I had just talked about sarcasm two hours before. As I listened to that husband, a sign flipped down on the chartboard of my mind. It read, "Discretion needed here."

Discretion means the quality of being careful or discreet about what one does and says. *Discreet,* in turn, means to be prudent, tactful, judicious, cautious, circumspect, diplomatic, and polite. Sarcasm falls far short of any of these meanings.

My personal definition of discretion is knowing when to speak and when to be quiet.

David makes an interesting statement in Psalm 39:1: "I will watch my ways and keep my tongue from sin; I will put a muzzle on my mouth as long as the wicked are in my presence." As I read this verse, an unusual picture flashed into my mind. A group of people dressed in their finest clothes stood around a room. And scattered among the crowd were a few people wearing contraptions that seemed totally out of place. I looked—then looked again. Some were actually wearing muzzles! I wondered if they were being punished in some way for speaking rashly against the others. But they wore them with dignity, heads held high. Then it dawned on me that these were *self-imposed muzzles* that could be removed at any time. I realized they were worn by those who were discreet consistently—those who did *not* say the wrong thing at the wrong time. I prayed then, "Lord, give me the wisdom and courage to *muzzle my mouth."*

A discreet person guards his lips, restrains his speech, and muzzles his mouth! One who has discretion has three endearing qualities: That person thinks before speaking, knows when to keep still, and understands when to speak.

Thinking before speaking seems to be a top priority in the Book of Proverbs. Before we speak, we are to *weigh our answers:* "The heart of the righteous weighs its answers, but the mouth of the wicked gushes evil" (Proverbs 15:28). On one side of the balance scales should be the question, Is it kind and true? and on the other side, Is it necessary? Often we would either be more wise in our responses or say nothing at all if we weighed our words on God's balance scales.

Not only should we consider our answers carefully, but we must give thought to what we do. In Proverbs 14:15 we are told, "A simple man believes anything, but a prudent man gives thought to his steps." In other words, a discreet person will not only think before he speaks, but before he takes action as well.

Undoubtedly, the most vivid verse for women is Proverbs 11:22, which says, "Like a gold ring in a pig's snout is a beautiful woman who shows no discretion." The same truth is found in Ephesians 5:4: "Nor should there be obscenity, foolish talk or coarse joking, which are out of place, but rather thanksgiving." We say so much that is out of place—the wrong thing at the wrong time or even the right thing at the wrong time.

In an interview, author and speaker Ann Kiemel Anderson said, "One of the qualities I long for more than anything is that I won't speak before I think and feel and understand and know what it is I'm supposed to say—that I won't react, but that I will respond . . . to my husband, to others and to experiences in life."[1]

Frank, a fireman, told us of a time when his unit was called to a shooting. He and his partner arrived before the police. Even though the shooting had been reported as a suicide, Frank went into the apartment slowly and found a man lying in the hallway. After the body had been removed, Frank chatted with the man who owned the apartment. In his nervousness, the owner complained, "He got blood all over my new carpet! I'm so mad, I could kill him!"

Then, as Frank was trying not to laugh, the man realized what he'd said and grinned sheepishly.

Esther, my roommate from college days who knows me

too well, sent me this quote: "Small thought: The biggest trouble with having the gift of gab is wrapping it up."

We need to think!

And, then, we must know *when to keep still*. Sometimes, we should say nothing.

I love the story of the little girl who came home from a neighbor's house where her little friend had died.

"Why did you go?" questioned her father.

"To comfort her mother," said the child.

"What could you do to comfort her?"

"I climbed into her lap and cried with her."

This small child knew, instinctively, when to be still.

Sometimes it seems we just have to say something. Perhaps it is an unconscious, or even conscious, desire to impress. A couple of years ago I wrote,

> I did it again, Lord,
>   And I'm sorry.
> You have convicted me before
>   about "name-dropping,"
>   "place-dropping,"
>   "knowledge-dropping."
> That wasn't the problem this time, Lord.
> In sharing around the table
> with a small group of dear Christians,
> I realized afterward
>   there was an inner desire
>   to impress.
> Oh, I didn't say anything I didn't mean.
> We shared about You, Lord,
>   and that was good.
> But somewhere in my being,
>   instead of sharing from an
>   overflowing heart,

I seemed to be sharing out
    of a need to impress by my
    "overflowing heart."
Forgive me, Lord!
Help me to keep silent
until You tell me to speak.

I want to be a woman of knowledge and understanding. But do you know some of the characteristics of such a person? "A man of knowledge uses words with restraint, and a man of understanding is even-tempered. Even a fool is thought wise if he keeps silent, and discerning if he holds his tongue" (Proverbs 17:27-28). When I read that, I thought of what my grandmother used to say: "Better to keep silent and be thought a fool than to open your mouth and remove all doubt!"

I have to confess that I have a hard time knowing when to be quiet. When there is a silence, I get uncomfortable and think I've got to fill it.

I'll never forget a wedding of dear friends at which Jack was to officiate. We arrived early at the farm and went into the large living room where about twenty members of the family and friends gathered to visit before going to the rehearsal. We sat on folding chairs in a circle. A silence fell over the group that went on . . . and on . . . and on.

So I started to talk. I chatted on like a radio. I could feel Jack's disapproval. The more I felt it, the more nervous I became. The more nervous I became, the faster I talked. After what seemed an interminable time, we got in our cars and headed for the church.

Jack drove, eyes straight ahead, not saying a word.

Finally, I broke the silence. "You think I talked too much," I stated feebly.

"Yes."

"Well," I explained, "nobody would say anything. I was trying to help them be comfortable."

Jack said, "Honey, they were comfortable. You were the one who was not."

A wise husband—and absolutely right. Those farm people knew each other well and were comfortable with the silences. I should have let them be comfortable instead of my being a chatterbox.

In this case I don't think I said anything offensive, but Proverbs 10:19 warns that "when words are many, sin is not absent." *The Living Bible* is just as clear: "Don't talk so much. You keep putting your foot in your mouth. Be sensible and turn off the flow!" In other words, if I talk long enough, I'm bound to say something I shouldn't! Then I'll be able to identify with the cartoon character Ziggy, who said, "I put my foot in my mouth so often, it's a wonder I don't have athlete's mouth!!"[2]

We need to learn to be quiet.

Finally, we need to learn when to speak. In Psalm 39:2 David laments, "When I was silent and still, not even saying anything *good,* my *anguish* increased" (italics mine).

Part of discretion is doing and saying things that are proper. For one period in my life, I did not like doing something just because it was "proper." But God changed that attitude as a result of reading the Word one day.

When Christ came to John the Baptist to be baptized, John was awestruck and reluctant at the same time. He knew he wasn't fit to untie the thongs of the Master's sandals, yet Christ asked to be baptized by him. To John's hesitancy, Christ answered, "Let it be so now; it is proper for us to do this to fulfill all righteousness" (Matthew 3:15). Then John consented.

Jesus had John baptize Him because it was the proper thing to do! Now if Christ Himself felt that observing the correct custom was important, how much more should I.

Because some customs are deemed "proper" in various cultures, I will offend if I don't learn what is acceptable. A prominent minister almost ruined his effectiveness in a Middle Eastern country by crossing his legs while seated on a platform and showing the sole of his shoe to a dignitary on the same platform. In that culture this action was a sign of disrespect, of which the minister was unaware.

Our daughter and son-in-law live in Mexico. They have had to discover who to give a hug to, who should receive a double handshake, who to give an extra kiss to, and when. At Feliz Navidad (Christmas), special hugs and kisses are appropriate. Lynn and Tim would appear cold if they neglected them.

Doing the right or proper thing is part of having discretion both in speech and actions. For the sake of simplicity of lifestyle, do I fail to dress properly for a church dinner? If I work with a person who feels strongly against dining at a restaurant on Sunday, do I go out anyway because I have no such conviction? When I visit a cathedral overseas, do I cover my head as is fitting in that country? Do we care enough to learn about these things and therefore be discreet?

As ambassadors for Christ, we need discretion desperately. Part of that discretion is speaking both what is proper and when it is necessary. Martin Luther King once said, "History will have to record that the greatest tragedy of this period of social transition was not the strident clamor of the bad people, but the appalling silence of the good people."[3] Silence is often taken for approval. Therefore, when we do not approve, it may be sin *not* to declare our convictions.

The Apostle James wrote, "To him that knoweth to do good, and doeth it not, to him it is sin" (James 4:17, KJV). I wonder how many times I have sinned by not writing a note of encouragement when God prompted me to do so, by not speaking up for a friend who was being criticized, or by not defending a principle in the arena of untruth.

You see, there are some matters we are commanded, or at least exhorted, to speak to. For instance, we are exhorted to *encourage* one another: "A man finds joy in giving an apt reply—and how good is a timely word!" (Proverbs 15:23). We are told to speak pleasant words that promote instruction and build Christ-like character into the lives of other people. We are to speak the truth in love and to encourage each other daily.

Solomon, the wisest man of all time, wrote that there is a time to speak as well as a time to be still (see Ecclesiastes 3:7). He also took time to search for just the right words when he spoke (see Ecclesiastes 12:10). May you and I not talk about where we have not yet walked. May we be real and genuine and honest. May we keep on learning the lessons about our words every day of our lives.

If you meet me two years from now, or even ten, and I make a blundering statement, please don't think, *And she wrote a book on the subject!* No. I am a person in process. God is chipping away at the peeling paint in my life, driving nails in where the boards are breaking away, and working hard to make my house what it should be. He is painting deep brush strokes in my life, but He has a long way to go.

> Pay attention to my wisdom, listen well to my words of insight, that you may maintain discretion and your lips may preserve knowledge. (Proverbs 5:1-2)

NOTES

1. Judith E. Torkildsen, "Talking with Ann Kiemel Anderson," *Virtue*, vol. 6, no. 4, March/April 1984, page 66.
2. © 1978 United Press Syndicate.
3. Martin Luther King, as quoted in "Quotable Quotes," *Reader's Digest*, vol. 124, no. 742, February 1984, inside front cover.

BIBLE STUDY APPLICATION

1. a. What comes to your mind when you think of a person who is discreet?

   b. How would you define the word *discretion*?

2. What do these verses say about what we say?

   a. Psalm 39:1

   b. Proverbs 10:19

   c. Proverbs 15:28

   d. Proverbs 17:27-28

   Using the thoughts of these verses, write a paragraph describing how a discreet person will talk.

3. a. Write Proverbs 14:15 in your own words.

   b. What are three ways this truth could be put into practice every week in your home?

4. a. According to Proverbs 5:1-2, how is discretion gained?

   b. What practical steps could you take this week to gain discretion?

⫷ 8 ⫸
"How Can You Say That!"
ON GIVING AND RECEIVING REPROOF

Jack was frowning as he began to speak. "Honey, there are two things I want to talk to you about concerning our time this evening."

Mentally, I winced. I must have done something wrong, and this was confirmed as he continued. "You talked too fast and you shouldn't have joked about one matter."

I bristled. Then I swallowed my bristles and said, "Sorry, I'll work on it." But inside I was saying, "That's not fair. Well, yes, the first comment is. I do talk too fast, and that's habitual, but this is the very first time I have joked about that subject. You know it isn't a tendency I have, so why are you being so picky?"

The fact that I still remember that incident twenty-five years later shows it really irked me. But deep inside I knew even then that Jack loved me and wanted to help me. And I wanted to be helped.

Or did I? Do I?

As we were having lunch together, my friend leaned halfway over the table and dropped her voice. "Carole," she said earnestly, "if you ever see anything about my life that isn't right, please tell me. I want you to know I am open to you."

I regarded her thoughtfully. Her sweet smile and intent expression made me realize she was sincere. But I still thought somewhere in the back of my mind, *Do you mean that?* And echoing along the hallways of my life was the question, When I say that to a friend or loved one, do I mean it?

It is probably most difficult to take correction from someone we love. Consciously or unconsciously, we think, *If they have observed that ugly thing about me, they must not like me. If they don't like me, how can they possibly love me the way I long to be loved?*

What do we do about correction? How do we receive it and how do we give it? At times it is actually easier to receive correction than to give it. I have observed that the person who has the gift of mercy often tries to avoid any kind of confrontation or conflict. (Mercy is a beautiful gift, but those who have it need extra grace to enable them to discipline, confront, and correct.) Some people seem to have no trouble at all confronting others. The ability to easily confront and reprove is called the gift of prophecy by some. Others say it is the choleric personality, or attribute it to a certain nationality. Some people can both rebuke others and take reproof without batting an emotion.

Many churches ignore it. Some Christians abuse it.

God, however, gets specific about it and has a lot to say about the hows and whys of giving and receiving reproof.

I know of a man who needed to talk to an employee who was doing a poor job in one area of work. The employer knew the man would have a million excuses for what he was doing. Since they were both Christians, the employer called his employee into his office and said, "John, let me read you Proverbs 15:31-32: 'He who listens to a life-giving rebuke will be at home among the wise. He who ignores discipline despises himself, but whoever heeds correction gains understanding.' Now then, I know you don't want to despise yourself or be a fool, so I'd like to talk to you about your work."

Perhaps not the most subtle approach. But in this case, it worked!

Let's talk about some dos and don'ts of receiving admonition. How should we handle it when someone comes to us with a fault they have observed in our life?

We should not bring up all the things we have observed about them! Instead, we must listen—with our mouth shut.

A friend of ours (I'll call him Jim) prayed for a number of weeks and then sought out Frank, a fellow-worker, to talk about something he had observed in Frank's life. Jim had no sooner started when Frank began to berate Jim on several things he had noticed.

Jim interrupted Frank and said, "Wait a minute, friend. How long have you observed these things about me?"

Frank said angrily, "Well, at least six months."

"Then," answered Jim, "you should have come to me about this long ago, and I would have listened. But right now, we need to discuss what I have on my heart to tell you."

Jim was right. He knew that Frank's outburst was a smokescreen of defensiveness. I repeat. We must listen with our mouth shut.

But we need to do more than that. We need to receive reproof with HOPE:

H umbly, with
O pen heart,
P rayerfully
E nduring without retaliation.

Hard? You bet! Impossible really, without the strength of the Holy Spirit within you.

I'd been leading a Bible study for several weeks, and was excited about the women who were digging into God's Word with me, when one member of the group phoned.

"Carole," she said, "a couple of the women in our study are considering dropping out."

Startled, I asked, "Why would they do that?"

"It's you," she said. "You intimidate them."

I sank into the nearest chair and managed to choke out, "How do I intimidate them?"

"You look at them so piercingly and ask such direct questions. You make them feel uncomfortable."

As I hung up, anger, pain, and frustration battled for position. But as I cried, God brought to mind some thoughts from His Book:

Do not reprove a scoffer, lest he hate you,
Reprove a wise man, and he will love you.
Give instruction to a wise man, and he will be still wiser,
Teach a righteous man, and he will increase his learning.
(Proverbs 9:8-9, NASB)

The wise of heart will receive commands,
But a babbling fool will be thrown down.
(Proverbs 10:8, NASB)

The way of a fool is right in his own eyes,
But a wise man is he who listens to counsel.
(Proverbs 12:15, NASB)

A fool rejects his father's discipline,
But he who regards reproof is prudent.
(Proverbs 15:5, NASB)

Then I prayed, "Father God, help me. This hurts. And the reproof is so vague, I can't get a handle on it. I'm not even aware of what I do that intimidates people. But I want to learn—I want to receive—I want to grow. So thank you for this, even if it hurts."

I don't think any of us want to be scoffers or babbling fools. We really do want to be wise, righteous, and prudent. So we must "listen good" and receive reproof quickly with a teachable heart, careful thought, and personal application (see Proverbs 4:13, 23:12, 24:32, and 29:1). Then *h*umbly, with *o*pen heart, *p*rayerfully *e*ndure . . . H O P E.

All right, you say. I'll listen. But what if not a word is true?

Whether it is or isn't, our response must be the same. Afterward, if the reproof is wrong, there will be a difference in what we do with it, but not at the time of confrontation. After listening, we need to say something like, "Thank you for sharing that with me. Let me pray about it and think it through."

You know, the person could be right. That's why humility is important. We must receive correction and take it before the Lord with an open heart, praying, "Lord, if there is the slightest truth to this, show me and change me. If there isn't, show me that, too. Then help me forget it and forgive the person who confronted me."

As I prayed over that phone call concerning the Bible

study, I had to do some deep soul-searching. I learned something about the hopelessness of trying to change an aspect in me without throwing myself on the One who made me; of confessing something I hadn't even been aware of; of learning to love someone who hurt me; of agonizing in prayer concerning an unlovely characteristic; and finally, of accepting the fact that some people won't like me no matter how hard I try. These are valuable lessons for a woman to learn—not that they were learned (past tense and final), but the process was begun.

If God shows you that the reproof is totally false, then, after praying for His mind and His wisdom, you may want to discuss it with the person. Or you may want to forgive and forget without responding. Remember, *God* will be your defense.

Two godly men in my past made it a policy *never* to come to their own defense. Both were accused of terrible and untrue things. But both felt that God had promised to be their defense, and they needed to leave it in His hands.

Now what about giving reproof? The Bible tells us that we are to "admonish one another" (Colossians 3:16). Most of us rarely practice that command. We have gone so far overboard on speaking with love that we neglect the fact that we are to speak the *truth* in love.

I have to confess that, being part sanguine (cheerful) and phlegmatic (easy-going), having a need to be accepted and liked, being a bit insecure, and knowing my own faults, I wrestle with the command to admonish. I struggle inside when God lays it on my heart to bring something to the attention of someone. I agonize. I procrastinate. I avoid it if at all possible. But I do *pray*. And that's the secret.

I think one of the greatest "how-to" verses in all of the Scripture on this subject is Galatians 6:1, which comes to my mind time and again: "Brothers, if someone is caught in a sin, you who are spiritual should restore him gently. But watch yourself, or you also may be tempted."

There are four specifics here.

First of all, Galatians 6:1 refers to *"brothers,"* fellow Christians. In other words, we don't rebuke, admonish, or restore unbelievers. The sin we need to talk about with them is their unbelief. To rebuke an unbeliever about his unlicensed behavior is futile. He needs Christ in order to even be open to conviction about something he is doing.

Second, the verse speaks about "someone . . . caught in a *sin*." (The *King James Version* says "fault," but the word means sin.) We need to ask ourself a question before we admonish someone: Is this something that the Bible specifically condemns? Is this sin?

A dear girl came to me one time weeping. She had just been told by another girl that the dress she was wearing was "sexy," and that she shouldn't wear clothes like that. She was full-figured and almost anything she wore could have been seen by some as "sexy." In the midst of her tears, she added, "But do you know that shortly after this girl told me my dress was too sexy, a Christian leader came by and casually said, 'What a beautiful dress!'"

Oh, dear friends, we should be extremely careful not to admonish someone because our *taste* is different or our lifestyles are opposite. We are often quick to judge personalities, personal preferences, characteristics, and habits. The Bible says we are to deal with *sin*. Frankly, it may be a *sin* of judging on our part if we don't limit ourself to those areas that are clearly sin.

The third important idea in Galatians 6:1 is *"you who are spiritual."* That phrase could easily stop me right there. Each of us could say, "I'll never talk to anyone about anything because there is so much wrong with me."

Years ago when we had several men living with us, Jack

felt he needed to talk to one concerning something in his life. But he hesitated, saying, "Al is the most consistent person I've ever known as far as spending time with God. You can set your watch by him. He gets up at 5:00 a.m. and walks the blocks praying for an hour each morning before he goes to work. How can I talk to him about anything when he is so much more consistent in this area than I am?"

Jack counseled with a godly leader, who said, "Jack, if I waited until everything in my life was perfect to talk to someone about his life—well, I would never talk to anyone about anything."

I think this verse means that if we are attuned with God, if we are not harboring any sin in our life, if we will approach the person in love and directed by God, if we listen to His voice as we speak, if we have prayed for words and wisdom, then we are spiritual, and free to restore. We are obeying God.

Fourth, this verse says about the sinner that we should "*restore him gently.*" But first, we should ask ourself, "Am I the one to restore this person?" Several questions need to be considered before we answer "yes" to the responsibility of restoring a fellow believer: Is this person open to me? Is the timing right? Is this my responsibility (as a teacher, elder, or older Christian)? Has it come to me through my position, the church, or God?

How do we restore a person gently? God's wisdom is essential. We must pray for it, for the right words, for graciousness, for a non-judgmental attitude, for the person's openness, for the right timing, and, above all, for love. Love will be evident to the person if we really have love. If we do, and say everything wrong, the person will respond to our love anyway. If we say everything right, but without love, the person is going to sense that as well.

Go to the person when your heart is loving, not angry

or judgmental. Perhaps you will need to rehearse your words out loud to the Lord first, or write them down and talk them over with a spouse or a friend you can trust. But then *go*. Solomon, king of Israel, wrote, "Faithful are the wounds of a *friend*" (Proverbs 27:6, italics mine). If we really are friends, we will be faithful to help one another stay on track in our spiritual lives, faithful to help one another grow and develop as we long to do.

The book in the Bible that has the most to say on this subject was written by the wisest man of all time. Solomon admonished, "He who ignores correction despises himself, and he who listens to reproof acquires intelligence" (Proverbs 15:32, MLB).

Galatians 6:1 ends with this warning: "But watch yourself, or you also may be tempted." We may be bothered most by seeing things in others that we struggle with in our own life. We may be extremely sensitive to the things in a brother's life that cause us great temptation. God says, "Be careful."

At times it may be necessary to admonish someone about things that are not specific sin. Your child's rude table manners are not a sin, but you hope to correct them to prepare the child for the expectations of society and to be a positive testimony in the world. You want to help friends with bad grammar (if they ask) and help your spouse overcome a poor habit.

I worked with a girl for several months, helping her in her walk with God. It was hard to talk with her because she had absolutely no facial responses when we conversed. I was distracted because I wondered constantly if anything I said was getting through. This discouraged me from trying.

She, in turn, was working with some other women to help them in their spiritual walk. One day, I began to wonder if her lack of facial expression was a hindrance to

HOW CAN YOU SAY THAT!

her effectiveness. Knowing some of the women she was working with, I asked them about this. They felt she wasn't enthusiastic about what she was teaching them, and they wondered if she really liked them. Knowing that her heart was full of love for the Lord and the girls, I prayed about talking to her.

As I studied Scripture and prayed, God showed me that her poor facial communication wasn't a sin, but it was something that Scripture spoke to in Proverbs 27:19: "As in water face reflects face, so the heart of man reflects man" (NASB). I thought about how we human beings respond to someone reflecting their expressions and responses back to us. On this basis, I talked to her about working on that aspect of her life. She listened and began to work on it, and our relationship deepened. A wise woman, that one.

Generally speaking, however, subjects that are not clearly sin should be left alone.

We may not have the wisdom of Solomon, but we have Christ, who is our wisdom. Knowing Him will help us become wise, and in that wisdom have the ability to both give reproof and correction, and to receive it from others as from the living God Himself.

BIBLE STUDY APPLICATION

1. a. Think of someone you consider to be wise. What in this person's life *demonstrates* wisdom to you?
   b. To what do you attribute this person's wisdom?
2. a. How are wisdom and understanding acquired, according to Proverbs 15:31-33?
   b. Take a few minutes to pray about these verses.
3. a. When was the last time you can remember being reproved by another Christian?
   b. How did you receive that reproof?

    c. When was the last time you brought something nega-
       tive to another person's attention (other than your
       children)?

    d. How did they receive the correction?

4. What do these verses say about reproof and correction?

    a. Proverbs 9:8-9

    b. Proverbs 12:15

    c. Proverbs 15:5

5. a. Write Galatians 6:1 in your own words.

    b. Can you think of a situation to which this verse should
       be applied?

9

"Easy Does It"

ON GENTLENESS

Gentleness.

The very word sounds as soft as a baby's touch. It brings to our mind the serenity of lapping waves on a secluded beach and the tenderness of a lover's first kiss.

Our granddaughter, Sunny, was born fast and has been gaining speed ever since. Being three years younger than her brother, Eric, who was almost six when they visited us one Christmas, she often followed him around, copying everything he did.

After being puppy-dogged all day long by his younger sister, Eric finally gave up in frustration. He stomped one foot, shrugged his shoulders hopelessly, and with his eyes about to brim over in tears he spurted, "Sunny does everything I do—only louder."

It is true. Sunny does everything Eric does—louder and faster and like a house on fire. Sunny, bless her, is going to have to *learn* gentleness.

Or is she?

For years I had a secret longing. I wanted to be a quiet, soft-spoken lady. In my mind, a lady was someone who was kind, calm, and tenderhearted. She was a serene person who never was awkward or ill at ease, who never spoke an angry word. She was like the heroine of George MacDonald's book *The Baronet's Song.* Of her he wrote,

> She was still the same small brown bird as of old. She had the sweetest, rarest smile—not frequent and flashing like Gibbie's, but stealing up from below, like the shadowy reflection of a greater light. Her atmosphere was an embodied stillness; she made a quiet wherever she entered. She was not beautiful, but she was lovely; and her presence at once made a place such as one would desire to be in.[1]

That was my mental picture of a lady. And then there was me, quite the opposite, I felt.

As I studied the Bible, I began to realize that the fruit of the Spirit listed in Galatians 5:22-23 are characteristics that God wants each of His children to have. And the list includes gentleness. Then I began to study some godly women around me, and I was shocked and delighted to find that some bubbly, outgoing, talkative women had quiet and gentle spirits. Conversely, I knew some women with calm personalities who had rebellious, stubborn hearts. Mentally, I breathed a sigh of relief.

I had interpreted 1 Peter 3:3-4 all wrong. It says, "Your beauty should not come from outward adornment, such as braided hair and the wearing of gold jewelry and fine clothes. Instead, it should be that of your inner self, the unfading beauty of a gentle and quiet spirit, which is of great worth in God's sight." A gentle *spirit* has nothing to do with one's *personality*. God created us with great diversity in our personalities, but each of us should have a quiet and gentle spirit. We can be loud on the outside and still be hushed on the inside.

The Lord Jesus said that He was "gentle and humble in *heart*" (Matthew 11:29). Yet He wanted both boisterous, impetuous Peter as well as loving John to emulate Him.

A number of synonyms for gentleness show us that it is not confined to one personality type—words such as *kindly, tender, peaceful, compassionate, tolerant, merciful, thoughtful,* and *considerate.* One can be loud and kindly, excitable and tender, bubbling and peaceful, talkative and compassionate, effervescent and considerate.

Some specific positions and situations demand gentleness. For instance, Paul told Timothy that an overseer must be "gentle, not quarrelsome" (1 Timothy 3:3). Paul, a leader of leaders, was an example to us in his gentleness toward the Thessalonians, "like a mother caring for her little children" (1 Thessalonians 2:7).

But just because we are not overseers, or akin to the Apostle Paul, we are not free of responsibility. We are to pray for God's wisdom (see James 1:5), and gentleness is a quality of that wisdom (see James 3:17). As servants of the Lord, we are to be gentle toward everyone (see 2 Timothy 2:24). According to Titus 3:2, we are to be peaceable and gentle to all men (including women).

Wives—especially those who have unsaved husbands—are to have gentle and quiet spirits: "Wives, . . . be submissive to your husbands so that, if any of them do not believe the word, they may be won" (1 Peter 3:1). The fact that an unbeliever may be won to the Lord is a pertinent reason for gentleness.

Sometimes translations of the Bible use the words *meekness* and *gentleness* interchangeably. But according to W. E. Vine in *Vine's Expository Dictionary of New Testament Words*, meekness has more to do with temperament or a habit of mind, and gentleness has more to do with action in dealing with others. In other words, gentleness is how we act as a result of being meek.[2]

The results of gentle speech are phenomenal! Leaders can be persuaded and hurts can be healed (see Proverbs 25:15 and 16:24). The truth that stands out to me is in Proverbs 15:1: "A gentle answer turns away wrath." And it works! Even when your motives are all wrong.

Just after my father died, I was home with my mother helping her take care of a number of things. One night I answered the phone for her, and the man at the other end, thinking I was Mother, started hollering and swearing at me. His dog had jumped the fence and attacked Mother's small Pomeranian, injuring her to the extent of needing surgery. Mother had called this man about it, but the man denied that his dog was the attacker. The second time, Mother reported it to the police, who paid the man a visit telling him to improve the fence. The man was furious and called Mother a number of times to berate her. This was one of those times.

I let the man rant on and on until at last he wound down. I was mad, too, by this time, but determined to try out Proverbs 15:1. So very gently and oh so softly, I said, "I am so sorry you feel that way, sir. Is there anything else you want to tell me?"

I could almost hear his surprise. He gasped, there was a long pause, and then he slammed down the phone. And he never called again!

It worked. Even when my motives were terrible.

If we were to analyze all the people we know that we could describe as gentle, some common denominators would be found. My list would go something like this:

1. Voice. A gentle person does not scream! A gentle answer turns away wrath partly because the tone must be soft, without rancor, not strident. (One translation of Proverbs 15:1 uses the word *soft*.) For some of us, this may mean asking God for extra control in difficult situations.

2. Facial expressions. An angry countenance, tight lips, a dour look—all convey a lack of gentleness.

3. Manner. A gentle person is kind, tolerant, and compassionate, thinking of other's feelings before he thinks of his own.

4. Attitude. A gentle person is unbiased, not bigoted or judgmental.

Gentleness cannot be melted down into one golden attribute. Each quality of gentleness remains distinct.

> Gentleness is strong, yet sweet;
>> tough, yet tender;
>> unwavering, yet merciful.
> Gentleness is not a shriek,
>> but a shimmer;
> not sharp,
>> but muted;
> not raucous,
>> but winsome;
> not rigid,
>> but controlled;
> not proud,
>> but prudent;
> not demanding,
>> but giving;

not brittle,
  but compassionate;
not grim,
  but joyful;
not clamoring,
  but quiet.

I have a feeling that many of life's difficulties are God's chisel to shape gentleness in our life. When a loved one was struggling with pain, I wrote,

May all the rough things she's going through
  be used to polish and perfect
  so she will more beautifully reflect You.
May the fine sandstone of pain
  polish rather than grind or irritate.
May she not try to tough it through
  in her own strength,
  but allow You to tenderize her spirit.
May she not become brittle under the pain—
  or bitter,
  but better—gentle, yielded,
  yet strong with Your strength.
Not hard or harsh,
  but teachable and tender.

We don't have an option to be gentle. God commands it. It is a fruit of the Holy Spirit who indwells us. We need to ask God for His Spirit to express His gentleness through us.

Does that sound hopeless to you who, perhaps like me, realize that gentleness is not a characteristic looming large in your life? Remember, my friends, that a godly woman is simply a sinner who is increasingly letting God *be* God in her life. She accepts the negative things about herself without bemoaning them. She realizes that she is a jar of clay (2 Corinthians 4:7), and that each jar has a different function, but each possesses a priceless treasure—Christ.

Did you get that? *Christ* is in us! Of course we are deficient. Of course we are inadequate to be—to do. We are constantly learning that we are worse than we thought we were, but also learning and feeling and knowing that in God's eyes we are perfect. God sent His own Son in the likeness of sinful man to be a sin offering for us so that all of God's requirements for righteousness would be fully met in us! (See Romans 8:4.) God sees us as perfect because we are wrapped in the righteousness of Jesus.

Because of Christ, God loves us totally right now. He couldn't love us any more than He does this minute no matter what we do, or don't do. We cannot earn His love. He gives it to us freely. And because we are His precious children, He takes the responsibility to make us like Jesus. He gets involved in the process of our becoming gentle.

Remember that! Our lack of gentleness is God's problem, as well as ours, and He will help us with it if we let Him.

I have been rereading *Hudson Taylor's Spiritual Secret*,[3] in which the missionary talks about the exchanged life, exchanging your life for the life of Christ in you. He discovered that being faithful is not as much in *trying* to be faithful, but in *looking to the faithful One.* Put *gentle* in there: Being gentle is not so much in trying to be gentle, but in looking to the gentle Savior—knowing Him deeply and intimately. Being gentle is gazing into His face until you become more and more like Him. God's Holy Spirit will fill us with gentleness as we contemplate Him.

Yes, Sunny.

You and me, too.

NOTES

1. George MacDonald, *The Baronet's Song* (Minneapolis, Minnesota: Bethany

House Publishers, 1983), page 167.
2. W. E. Vine, *Vine's Expository Dictionary of New Testament Words* (Nashville, Tennessee: Royal Publishers, Inc., 1952), page 475.
3. Moody Press, 1979.

BIBLE STUDY APPLICATION

1. How would you define the word *gentleness?*

2. a. Read 1 Peter 3:3-4 out loud. Who comes to your mind when you read the words *gentle and quiet spirit* (NIV)?

    b. How else would you describe this person?

    c. How would you describe your spirit? Why?

    d. What do you think would make you more gentle?

3. a. Write 2 Timothy 2:24 in your own words.

    b. To whom does this verse apply?

    c. What are some ways you can practice being gentle
    with children?
    with a friend?
    with your marriage partner?
    with someone you don't get along with?

4. Take a few minutes to ask God for ways to work on the characteristic of gentleness. Choose two things that you can do this week to practice gentleness.

⁓ 10 ⁓
The Sacrifice of Praise

One of the biggest disappointments of my life came last summer. Jack and I were in Great Britain for some conferences. Then we planned to celebrate our thirty-fifth wedding anniversary with a two-week trip in southern England. For several years we had prayed about having our daughter and her husband join us overseas, and this looked like the perfect time. As we prayed, it seemed as though God opened doors, providing the money and the time for them to join us. Jack and I spent many hours poring over maps and hotel brochures to plan the perfect trip. We counted the days until they would arrive.

Two days before we were to drive to Birmingham,

England, to meet their plane, Lynn called. Tim was in the hospital with a stubborn kidney stone that necessitated surgery and resulted in infection and weakness for several weeks. Our plans and dreams were smashed to smithereens.

I sat in the huge bathtub at the huge conference center and cried . . . and cried . . . and cried. But between sobs I said, "I *will* praise You, Lord. I don't understand this—it doesn't seem right or good or kind or anything that I know You are. But I *will* praise You." And with tears mixing with the bathwater, I sang, "Praise to the Father, praise to the Son."

I am becoming more and more convinced that telling people about Christ is not the most important ministry we have in this life. Neither is feeding the hungry. Nor helping people find a deeper relationship with God. All of those things are important, and all are commanded by God.

But more and more I am persuaded that what pleases the heart of God most are the choices we make that no one sees but God—those everyday moments when God is the only audience; when we offer to Him the sacrifice of praise; when the sweet aroma of our thanksgiving reaches Him.

We are told to love the Lord our God with all our heart, soul, mind, and strength. But most of the time we can't get all four in tune at the same time. In the bathtub that June evening, I wasn't praising God with all my heart. It took several weeks for my emotions to harmonize with my will. But I was praising Him with all my mind and all my soul—and it was taking all my strength to do it.

When all joy is breaking loose in our life, we praise God with our heart, our mind, and our soul, but it doesn't take all our strength to do it. At that time, it's easy. But when our emotions are all negative, when circumstances make us want to scream—*then* praising God takes all our strength. And often our heart doesn't follow until later.

When we stand before the throne of God, somehow I don't think He is going to say, "Thanks, Carole, for leading that Bible study, for writing that book, for going to the nursing home." Instead, I think His "Well done, thou good and faithful servant" will be spoken—or not spoken—when He recalls all the hidden moments of my life: the times I was tempted to grumble and complain; when I wanted to say, "Hey, that's not fair! You didn't work that out the way I wanted You to"; the moments I said, "I will praise You, Father. I don't understand, but I will thank You. I love You."

The sacrifice of praise is the *fruit of our lips* according to Hebrews 13:15. This is the sweet, delightful fruit that we Christ-ones can offer to God. It is something we can actually do for our Father, something that pleases and gladdens Him.

Instead of all the negative, ugly words that come out of our mouth, may the secret daily moments of our heart be filled with praise. If they are, our speech will overflow as a sacrifice upon the altar of a living, loving God.

BIBLE STUDY APPLICATION
1. Read Hebrews 13:1-16 aloud, slowly. Write verse 15 in your own words.
2. In one or two sentences, write the main thought of verses 7-14.
3. a. Write the thought of verse 16 in a short sentence.
   b. Look up in a concordance two or three other verses about praise and write them down.
   c. Write down any problems or difficulties you see in Hebrews 13:16.
   d. How do you think God wants you to apply this verse this week? Be specific.

(You can use this method with any verse, but it is especially meaningful with verses you want to memorize.)

May God bless you richly as you study and grow. And may you and I never stop learning what God has for us in regard to that most troubling of all members—our tongue.